Statements take ....report or investigation documents:

"*ROBBINS advised agents that WILLIAMS took them to his music studio where they partied for a while. ROBBINS stated WILLIAMS had approximately 30 pounds of marijuana in a little bar area off of the studio. ROBBINS also advised agents that 'MEECHIE' and 'SHAQ' worked for WILLIAMS, and were very close to WILLIAMS.*"
—Ricky ROBBINS, Friend of Demetrius Thomas
(Interviewed by TFA DAVID FAGAN)

"*WIMBLEY stated he knew Sherman WILLIAMS. WIMBLEY and WILLIAMS played football together at the University of Alabama in Tuscaloosa, Alabama. WIMBLEY and WILLIAMS resided in the athletic dormitory. WIMBLEY told Agents he had seen WILLIAMS smoke marijuana while at the University and while in the dormitory. WIMBLEY stated he had never seen WILLIAMS sell marijuana.*"
—Prince Wimbley, Former University of Alabama football player, 1988 – 1992 (Interviewed by TFA ANTHONY C. CALDERARO)

"*WILLIAMS told SPIKES he was not afraid of being caught because no one ever checked the football players or their luggage. SPIKES stated he saw the marijuana, and had even purchased some from WILLIAMS once they returned to Tuscaloosa.*"
—Irving Spikes, Former University of Alabama football player ,1989-1992 (Interviewed by TFA ANTHONY CALDERARO)

i

"BUTLER told TFA CALDERARO she had received a telephone call from Prince WIMBLEY on the day Sherman WILLIAMS was arrested. WIMBLEY was calling on behalf of Kenneth RICE. WIMBLEY requested a telephone number so that RICE could contact WILLIAMS."

—Christina Lee Butler, Friend of Tasma Scott (Interviewed by TFA ANTHONY C. CALDERARO)

"COLSTON advised that SHERMAN WILLIAMS had the following people transporting marijuana for him: DEMETRIUS SANDERS, BOBBY RANDER, JR., DEMETRIUS THOMAS and RODERICK WARD. WARD went to prison on a drug charge for WILLIAMS. He used to drive WILLIAMS's Lexus. After WARD was released from prison, he went back to transporting drugs for WILLIAMS."

—Shamirrah Andreece Colston, Girlfriend of Demetrius Thomas (Interviewed by SA DANA R. RIDENOUR)

"SIMMONS was given $1,000 in $100 counterfeit bills for dancing that night. SIMMONS stated that JUICE pulled all the money out of his shirt pocket, and he was the one to give her the money. SIMMONS did not know where the money came from, or where it was stored. JUDKINS held the money for SIMMONS during the dance, and received $100. SIMMONS turned the money over to the United States Secret Service when she discovered it was counterfeit."

—Kay Simmons, Exotic Dancer (Interviewed by SA DANA RIDENOUR)

To SHELLY

BOOKS BY SHERMAN WILLIAMS:

Crimson Cowboy
Peace Between the Lines

PEACE BETWEEN THE LINES

PEACE BETWEEN THE LINES

Sherman Williams

Palmer Williams Group Media
Mobile, Alabama

DEDICATION

To my mother, Betty Ruth York Williams

During this whole entire ordeal, my mother never missed a beat. Before I was ever anybody, she always reminded me I was somebody.

Her love and affection was contagious. Even after her death, her presence is felt by many. People walk up to me regularly, and remind me of her character and demeanor. She was a fine, faithful, Christian woman who always taught the principle of right and wrong.

This is my first opportunity to offer a public apology to my mother . . .

Mother, I apologize.

R.I.H.

Sentencing

DECEMBER 7, 2000
UNITED STATES OF AMERICA (plaintiff) vs.
SHERMAN WILLIAMS (defendant)

THE CLERK: Case set for sentencing, Criminal 200067, United States versus Sherman Williams. Is the government ready?

MS. GRIFFIN: Ready to proceed.

THE CLERK: Is the Defendant ready?

MR. CLARK: Yes, Sir, I'm ready. I want to apologize to the Court—I didn't realize I would be in trial today until about an hour ago.

THE COURT: That's fine—thank you, Mr. Clark.

THE COURT: Counsel, wait a moment, if you will. There are two objections I thought I would make some tentative findings on. Then, I'll hear what response counsel may have, either by way of additional argument, or if there is any evidence you wish to offer.

On the first objection dealing with the base offense-level calculation, contending the amount of cocaine involved in the unsuccessful cocaine transaction that took place. I don't have the exact date, but Frank Freeman testified about it. Tentatively, the court finds that by a preponderance of the evidence, the attempted purchase of two kilograms of cocaine was attempted. And, under 1(b) 1.3 (a), two were acts and a part of the same course of conduct as the counts of conviction. So, tentatively, that objection would be denied.

Regarding the objection dealing with the two-point enhancement for the possession of a firearm by a co-defendant—I know Counsel is aware this court takes a very narrow view of that enhancement, and often does not apply it. However, in reviewing my bench notes I took in this case, it appears to me this is one of those cases when that narrow interpretation may not be warranted. So, preliminarily— tentatively—I found, by a preponderance of the evidence, has been established that the weapon did belong to the defendant, as testified to. Or, at least, had been his gun or in his possession as testified to by Roderick Ward. That gun was in the defendant's Marquis automobile that was used for one of the marijuana purchases when that automobile was stopped on March 2nd, and the gun was seized. According to Demetrius Thomas, that gun had been used by Mr. Sanders who was on that trip. Under the four-prong test in the 11th Circuit of that enhancement's applying, the gun would fall under all the elements of that four-prong test. In the court's judgment, it should be held attributable to the defendant.

So, first, I will hear any response the defendant wishes, evidence, or testimony to make to those tentative findings, and, I will hear from government.

MR. MADDEN: The first point, with respect to the cocaine, we stand on . . .

THE COURT: Mr. Madden, just for the record—clearly, I was looking for the four-prong test that's in a number of cases. One, where it's clearly stated in U.S. vs. Gallow, 195 fed 3rd 378, the possessor of the firearm was a co-conspirator. The possession was in furtherance of the conspiracy. The defendant was a member of the conspiracy at the time of the possession. Sanders and Ward were reasonably foreseeable by the defendant under the facts as I found them.

MR. CLARK: I think the . . . it's going to the gun—as I understood the presentence report—it wasn't Ward or Sanders. It was Thomas and Sanders.

THE COURT: Perhaps, I said Ward. Excuse me for interrupting, Mr. Madden, but I want to be doubly sure of my bench notes. I may have tabbed it at the wrong place. Thomas and Sanders—you are correct. Thomas is who testified on March 2nd, 2000—he and Sanders were driving the defendant's Marquis. If I said Ward, I stand corrected.

MR. MADDEN: So, the only testimony . . .

THE COURT: Excuse me. Ward saw the gun—that same gun—Exhibit 37, and saw the defendant with it. That was Ward's testimony in connection with the gun.

MR. CLARK: Now, what is happening is Thomas and Sanders are in the car that gets stopped. Sanders is dead. He didn't testify. Thomas testified he didn't know there was a gun in the car. So, the only living testimony was that Thomas didn't know the gun was there. That was elicited on direct testimony from the government.

THE COURT: No, he said he saw Sanders put it under the seat.

MR. MADDEN: He didn't know it was in the car until the stop. When they were in the car, he didn't know the gun was in the car. He saw the gun when the police were stopping them. He saw Ward—no, Sanders—get it out. So, as far as Thomas was concerned, the gun was unrelated to the marijuana in the trunk because he didn't even know it was there.

THE COURT: But, he said Sanders did.

MR. MADDEN: He said Sanders got it out. Now, Sanders—we don't know. He said, "I don't know who put it there," and that was the testimony. I think your notes reflect that.

THE COURT: He did.

MR. MADDEN: So, the only living witness said, "I don't know who put it there. I didn't know it was there." We are stopped. Sanders takes the gun, and puts it under the seat.

THE COURT: Which gun Ward says was the defendant's gun.

MR. MADDEN: But, you have to—I think you have to take the next step if you are going by vicarious liability because it's the possession of a gun by a co-conspirator. You have to look at jointly undertaken activity.

THE COURT: This is one of those mixed cases—which is a rare one—in that one could almost equally and strongly argue it was possession of the gun by the defendant, being constructive possession by the people, that drove the car he loaned to them with the gun in it.

MR. MADDEN: The gun was in the car when he loaned it, and the purpose of that is where it breaks down. If this were an ordinary civil case and you had to find by a preponderance of the evidence, I don't think you can make that leap and say, "Well, since it was in the car then—and, Thomas didn't know it was there—it must have been out in the car . . .

THE COURT: By the defendant.

MR. MADDEN: By Williams in furtherance of the transaction. That's an inference I don't think the government proved by a preponderance. They proved the opposite. If Thomas is a member of the drug conspiracy and charged with transportation of marijuana—which was their theory— he would have known, or would have been told. Yeah, there is a gun there that has something to do with the drug transaction. And, unambiguous testimony is he didn't know that.

THE COURT: Let me hear from the government on that before you go to the second point. Ms. Griffin?

MS. GRIFFIN: Your Honor, the car was given to Thomas and Sanders by the defendant, and is the testimony. Even though it was in his girlfriend's car, he is the owner of it. Both Sanders and Thomas are co-conspirators, even though Sanders is, of course, deceased. And, I think, either way the court looked at it, clearly by a preponderance, we connect this as being reasonably foreseeable. We proved the presence of it. I think the burden shifts at this point to the defense to show that it was improbable that it was connected to the drug activity.

MR. MADDEN: I can do that. If the reason for the gun was to protect the drugs, the person with the drugs would know the gun was there.

THE COURT: But, Sanders was with the drugs. He is not here to testify. He is not here to testify, but we have—and, I believe, the testimony of Thomas—that he saw Sanders. And, therefore, Sanders knew the gun was in the truck—he either took it out of the glove compartment, or put it under the seat in furtherance of the conspiracy to move the marijuana. I say this, Mr. Madden—I think we are going to start arguing back and forth with each other. You should be making the final point as Bill O'Reilly says on the O'Reilly Factor, "I will give the final point. Go ahead."

MR. MADDEN: The final point is this is one of those rare cases when rather than speculating what is reasonable and foreseeable, you see what the co-defendant—the co-conspirator—said. And, he said, "I didn't know it was there."

THE COURT: Okay.

MR. MADDEN: So, this proves the other point . . .

THE COURT: The court's final finding is that this adjustment is appropriate for the reason I stated. Do you wish to be heard on the cocaine points?

MR. MADDEN: We rest on the record.

THE COURT: Alright. Those objections, having been dealt with, the court would adopt the presentence report as prepared, and its findings that the criminal history is a one—the offense level is a thirty-four. As to Count One, the guideline is a hundred and fifty to a hundred and eighty-eight months. The statutory maximum, as to Counts Two and Four, is sixty months. And, the statutory maximum as to Count Five is a hundred twenty months. Are there any additional objections to those findings by the court?

MR. MADDEN: No, Sir.

THE COURT: Let me first hear from the prosecution, then I will hear from counsel and Mr. Williams. Ms. Griffin?

MS. GRIFFIN: Your Honor, the defendant has had a lifetime of opportunities that many other people have not had. It is unfortunate he chose this as his lifestyle. Clearly, he was not forced to do it. Clearly, he was not starving. Clearly, he did not need to do this. He was capable of doing many other things. He never stopped. Not when his first runner was caught, not when his second runner was caught, not when his third runner was caught. But for these changes, we contend he would still be dealing dope. He could have done many other things. There was no reason for this behavior. He chose this lifestyle. There is nothing having to do with this case or the trial that would merit his receiving a low-end sentence. In fact, to the contrary—we ask the judge for the high end of the guidelines.

THE COURT: Alright. Mr. Clark and Mr. Madden, if you will come up with Mr. Williams, I will hear from any and all of you. First the attorneys, whoever wishes to be heard.

MR. CLARK: Yes, Sir, Judge. You know, Ms. Griffin says he chose this lifestyle. It's a tragedy all the way around. You didn't get to know his mother, but, you know, she is here in court with him today. She attended every football game he ever played—every single one from little league to the present. She has been there with him and beside him and maintained employment throughout her lifetime. She is a perfect role model.

Now, having said that, Mr. Williams chose the wrong lifestyle. What we are looking for here is he has been convicted and the court is to pass sentence. But, we are also asking for mercy, Judge. The sentence in this case—I know the Sentencing Commission has passed this—but, if you look at what was going on at the time, we are talking about fifty pounds of marijuana. Yet, they want to put him in jail for about thirteen and a half years. A hundred fifty-one—a hundred forty-four month—is twelve years. A hundred and fifty-six is thirteen years. You know, it satisfies, I think, everybody's needs if you punish him, but, punish him with well-deserved mercy.

This is a good individual. He is a good man, Judge. "A good a man," James Carville said, "who did a bad thing. But, still, don't take his manhood away from him—he is still a good man, and still can be productive to this society." It's vindictive in the worse sense to say he deserves fifteen or sixteen years, Judge. He doesn't deserve it. The low end of the guidelines are extremely high—extremely, extremely high. I know you didn't promulgate them. I didn't promulgate them. But, I think you can take into consideration how high these guidelines are. And, you know, he is being punished for a lot of things that the prosecution didn't prove beyond a reasonable doubt. He is being punished for the cocaine. He's being punished for the gun. All of these are enhancements that will take, probably, an eight year sentence, and jack it up to twelve and a half or thirteenth years. We ask, Your Honor—beg, Your Honor—to please sentence him at the low end of the guidelines so it sends the message. The low end of the guidelines sends the news. They are Draconian. Can we keep doing this forever? Sentencing young men to forever in prison? I ask you to use reason, Judge, and mercy when sentencing Mr. Williams.

THE COURT: Alright. Mr. Madden, do you wish to be heard in addition?

MR. MADDEN: The only other thing—you have read letters, and I am sure you have. We, Deborah, and I, looked at them. It's unusual for—to have people who work at the jail as guards—write a letter. I don't think you see that very often. There are a number of them. And, if the court is concerned, as I think it should be, about what happens in the year 2012 or 2015—whenever the day will come when Sherman Williams will be on the street. I think you take some comfort in the fact when he was locked up after this occurred, he made the most of what opportunity he had down there—at least from what the guards report in their letter to you. I think that is a reason to exercise your discretion, and go with the low end of those guidelines. That is another reason.

THE COURT: Okay, then. Mr. Williams, this is your opportunity now, if you wish to be heard by the court. I will be glad to hear anything you want to offer on your own behalf.

THE DEFENDANT: Yes—I would like to say I feel blessed today to have my family here—to have my friends— showing me so much support throughout these troubled times. And, I want to show my sincere gratitude to my mother for standing by me through everything. My father for being here today. My other friends—David Palmer, and my fiancé, Tasma Scott. I am just blessed to be here today, and in front of you to express these feelings. It's an unfortunate situation for me to be faced with such difficult circumstances. But, I understand, and I use this time to express my sincere remorse for any wrong doing I have done. But, there have been some things that have been said about me that just aren't true. At the same time, I feel like this experience has took my life from one extreme to another. But, I know it's through God's grace, I will be strong. I will make it through. I will come out, and I will be a better person. I want to say thank you, and may God bless America.

THE COURT: Mr. Williams, I can assure you this is one of the toughest cases I have probably ever had before me. Because I am dealing with somebody who stands as a fallen hero. A hero in a lot of people's eyes.

Not just football fans for whom you were that hero, including this judge, who can remember standing and cheering many a time when you made some great run for the University of Alabama. But, for all of those people in your community that you stood out there as a hero for—

somebody who could climb out of your background, your broken home, and your relatively poor upbringing, and set an example. Just think of all of these people who looked up to Sherman Williams.

The tragedy is many of those same people are here today, still supporting you, for which I applaud them. I think it's wonderful, and I think it is, indeed, an incredible testimony to the strength you shared with them—and, they have with you—for everything that is good about you.

But, you stood that game and that hero status on its head. You absolutely turned it upside down. How you made that turn or where you made that wrong turn, I don't know, and I don't know why. But, I suspect money, greed, and selfishness had a lot to do with it.

I know your mother didn't bring you up to do that. I know that your mother, who went to every football game with you and supported you throughout your whole career, was not with you on a single marijuana transaction that you engaged in. Because you would have been ashamed to have her there. You stood that on its head, that life, and that support she gave you all of those years.

It is tragic and very hard for me, the judge, to do what I think the law provides for in this case. You've got these hundreds of people who have supported you, and that speaks a lot to me, Mr. Williams—that means a lot to me. But, this is not Bryant Denny Stadium. Those people cannot cheer you on to run across that goal line one more time.

You had your day on the field, and in the courtroom. And, the jury ruled you stepped out of bounds—you stepped way out of bounds. I want you to know, I listened to every word of testimony, and I looked at every exhibit. I reviewed it over and over again to see if there were some way I could say the best thing to do in this case is send a message to the community that if a hero falls, he doesn't have to fall very hard—he can get the low end of the guidelines because he was a hero.

Well, I think that would be standing the law on its head. I think the law requires—not requires, demands, cries out for justice. To say when someone like you betrays the confidence of all those coaches, all of those friends, all of that family, all those people who looked up to you and, in effect, says, "I don't want anything to do with that kind of living. I want to live with my drug dealing friends. I want to make this fast money. I don't care what this marijuana does that I sell to the community. I don't care how many homes it breaks up. I don't care how many teenagers get hooked on marijuana that I sell, whose careers I may have ruined. I don't care if their parents are spending their money on marijuana, and not supporting their kids.

That's the Sherman Williams who stands before me now—not the football hero. I wish it were just the football hero. I would be giving you a trophy if that's who you were. But, you're not Mr. Williams—you're a criminal who chose a deep, dark path to your destruction.

The message I have to send to the community—to the public, and all of those people—is there can be no excuse for what you did. You cannot step out of these circumstances you committed to, and hang on one more time to those glory days you lived for so long. You have set that past behind you, Mr. Williams, and you will serve a lengthy sentence in the Bureau of Prisons. Because, in my judgment, the only sentence appropriate is the top of the guidelines. You earned the best. One hundred and eighty-eight months in the Bureau of Prisons as to Count One. A concurrent sentence as to Counts Two and Four of sixty months custody. And, as to Count Five, a concurrent one hundred and twenty months. A total sentence of one hundred eighty-eight months.

Upon your release from that sentence, you will be placed on supervised release for a period of four years as to Count One. And, three years as to each of the other counts, to run concurrent, for a total of four years.

I'm not going to impose a fine because you have paid a substantial amount of restitution. But, you must pay the one hundred dollar special assessment as to each of those four counts.

You will have a long time to think about this. I am going to think about it more, too. And, I can tell you I probably will never forget it. As I said in the very beginning, this is very difficult for me to do. But, I know that, prayerfully, what I am doing is the right thing that justice requires.

When you are on supervised release you cannot commit any other state, federal, or local crimes. You must abide by all the standard conditions of release on file with this court. You cannot possess any firearms, dangerous weapons, or controlled substances. And, you are going to participate in whatever program of community service is deemed appropriate by the probation office. You'll take this difficult lesson you learned in life, and go back into the school system in Mobile to be available for whatever program can be fashioned for you—and, you, specifically. You'll reach out to those young kids, twelve, thirteen, and fourteen—who may then be the children of the people you sold marijuana to. Tell those kids how not to do what you did. How to take opportunity, and keep it heads up—not stand it on its head like you did. You will perform that community service during the period of time that you are on supervised release.

You have ten days from today if you wish to file a Notice of Appeal. And, Counsel, I will ask you now if either of you have any additional objections, other than these stated, to any of the Court's findings, conclusions, or the manner in which the sentence was imposed?

MR. MADDEN: No, Sir.

THE COURT: This matter is concluded, and Court is adjourned.

THOUGHTS

F aith is an interesting thing—jail was worse than I thought it might be, although I never really considered the possibility of spending time there. But, as I prepared for my trial, the seriousness of my situation dug in like a tick, and I knew I had to make a decision—accept the situation, knowing God was always with me, or give up.

I chose to accept the situation.

As days prior to the trial trickled by, it bothered me I wasn't going to look my best—the food in jail was worse than I imagined, and I gained weight no matter how much I tried to keep a decent physique by regular exercise. My attorney stressed the importance of my dressing conservatively, but it was a good bet my custom-made suits weren't going to fit. That was a considerable source of stress for me because before landing in jail, I was a man who prided himself on being well-groomed, as well as well-dressed. My attorney also advised shaving my facial hair, which I did. Terrible barber.

Between the suit issue and the bad shave, the thought of appearing before a judge and jury not looking my best was something I didn't want to deal with—but, I had to.

The day before the trial, I admitted to myself I was guilty of some charges—but, not all—and the truth about the mess I got myself into smacked me right between the eyes. I was being accused of things I didn't do, but there was nothing I could do.

The stage was set.

I also questioned my decision of bringing Robert Clark on as my defense attorney, but it was too late to make a change. So, again, I turned to the Lord to give me strength, peace, and acceptance. I was a firm believer in whatever happened was a part of His plan, and it was up to me to have the grace and dignity to get through the coming days. In those moments, I reflected on what Jesus went though during His trial, and how I could muster the same strength and understanding. I read the Bible daily in an effort to prepare myself, but I confess . . .

It was difficult.

Then—the first day.

Everything was surreal as prison guards transported me to the courthouse. Of course, I knew a little of what to expect—the prosecuting attorney's determination to achieve a guilty verdict on all charges was the main thing. And, I still wondered if my attorney were up to the challenge of defending me. I still wasn't sure . . .

All I could do was hope—and, pray.

THE FIRST DAY

DECEMBER 4, 2000

UNITED STATES OF AMERICA (plaintiff) vs.
SHERMAN WILLIAMS (defendant)

ATTORNEYS' OPENING STATEMENTS

MS. GRIFFIN: Well, I started to say good morning, but, by now, it's good afternoon . . . As I told you earlier, my name is Deborah Griffin, and I will be presenting this case to you along with Patsy Dow for the United States. The court told you the United States bears the burden of proof—we welcome that burden, and we contend we will show you that burden has been met by the end of this case.

We will ask you to listen carefully.

You'll hear from witnesses who participated in Sherman Williams's drug organization. You will hear from witnesses he hired—people to pick up marijuana for him. You will see the marijuana, and you will hear from the trooper who made some of the traffic stops, seizing some of the marijuana. You will see phone calls, you will see photographs, and you will hear live testimony from individuals who worked with and for Sherman Williams.

In this case, you will see Roderick Ward was a childhood friend of Sherman Williams, and Roderick Ward would go to Dallas when Sherman Williams played for the Cowboys. Roderick Ward learned Sherman Williams was buying marijuana, and Roderick Ward made a decision he needed to be the one who dealt with the marijuana dealers for his friend, Sherman Williams.

On the day Sherman Williams was cut from the Dallas Cowboys and was no longer a football player, Roderick Ward met with the drug dealer, purchasing marijuana with Sherman Williams's money for Sherman Williams. He brought that marijuana from Dallas to Mobile where he sold it, and he took the money back to Sherman Williams who no longer had a job.

You will hear Roderick Ward tell you on several occasions, he made this trip for his childhood friend, Sherman Williams—he will tell you the money was Sherman's. He will tell you the drugs were Sherman's—and, he will tell you the profits were Sherman's.

You will hear from Demetrius Thomas, who will tell you he made one trip from Mobile to Dallas with Roderick Ward when they picked up marijuana for Sherman Williams. You will hear he made trips by himself. And, you will hear he was caught on March 2nd of 2000 in Mobile with three pounds of marijuana, and a gun belonging to Sherman Williams. He was caught in Sherman Williams's girlfriend's vehicle, a vehicle Sherman Williams gave him.

You will hear Demetrius Thomas was stopped in Texas, yet again running drugs for Sherman Williams. You will see the drugs taken on that occasion, and you will hear Demetrius Thomas tell you about working for Sherman Williams in the drug business.

You will not hear from Demetrius Sanders. He died in April of 2000. You will hear the other witnesses tell you Demetrius Sanders, too, made drug trips for Sherman Williams, some of them with the individuals named on the screen.

You will hear from Frank Freeman, who will tell you he, too, is a childhood friend of Sherman Williams, and he will tell you he made four drug trips for Sherman Williams. He made three when they sort of went their separate ways and, after some of these other people were arrested, he made one last trip of 2000—he was stopped in Texas.

You will see the video where Frank Freeman tells a Texas trooper he's running dope for Sherman Williams. You will hear Frank Freeman tell you he agreed to bring that dope with the law enforcement back to Mobile in the Volkswagon Jetta Sherman Williams gave him to use to transport the marijuana—and, to tape Sherman Williams picking up the dope. Law enforcement officers got in the Jetta Sherman Williams gave Frank Freeman, and they drove from Texas to where they turned over the car, drugs, and Frank Freeman to the Mobile officers.

You will hear the Mobile officers took the dope Frank Freeman had when he was stopped with the marijuana he got for Sherman Williams—and, he put it in Frank's apartment. They set Frank's apartment up with video equipment, and you will hear Frank Freeman placed telephone calls to Sherman Williams to inquire about what time Sherman Williams would pick up the drugs.

Sherman Williams was in Dallas when Frank Freeman left Dallas. Sherman Williams did not carry the drugs on his person—rather, Frank Freeman was hired to do that by Sherman Williams.

You will hear Sherman Williams comes to Mobile, and you will see a video where he goes to Frank Freeman's house, handling each of the pounds of marijuana. He holds them up, and pinches—or, takes off the top of each pound—to make two smaller bags. You will see and hear him talking about his drug organization.

You will see Sherman Williams leave Frank Freeman's residence with the bags of marijuana. He put them in the Jetta and, as he prepared to leave, you will hear officers tell you they attempted to stop him. They identified themselves as police officers. They were dressed as police officers, and Sherman Williams ran. You will hear but for his tripping over a guide wire, he probably would still be on the run.

You will hear when he ran from law enforcement, he tossed the two bags he topped off—or, pinched—out of the pound. And, you will hear he was arrested on the twenty first of April of this year.

You will hear from Demetric Beans, who is an exotic dancer or stripper, and she was a sexual acquaintance of Sherman Williams. She let individuals come to her residence in Texas to pick up marijuana for Sherman Williams, and she provided a safe haven for her lover, Sherman Williams, who sent his runners to pick up marijuana. You will hear she knew Roderick Ward was to pick up for Sherman Williams, and she knew Demetrius Thomas was to pick up drugs for Sherman Williams. She knew Demetrius Sanders was to pick up for Sherman Williams, and she knew Frank Freeman was to pick up for Sherman Williams.

The case you have before you involves four counts—

the court told you briefly what they were. There are four charges—the first charge is conspiracy, and it covers Sherman Williams and all of these individuals. It's the count that encompasses the entire time from beginning to the end.

The second count involves a fourth stop of Demetrius Thomas in Texas with fifty pounds of marijuana he got for Sherman Williams.

The third count involves the March 2nd stop of Demetrius Thomas when he is in Sherman Williams's girlfriend's car—he had Sherman Williams's marijuana, and the gun provided by Sherman Williams.

The fourth count is the April 20th stop in Texas of Frank Freeman with the fifty pounds he was transporting to Mobile for Sherman Williams.

At the end of the case, I will have the opportunity to argue those counts, what we believe the evidence shows, and the court will give you instructions you are to apply to the evidence you will hear.

Ladies and Gentlemen, we are going to try to present this in order. Naturally, because some of these people were making trips about the same time, we will call them and go through all of their trips at one time before we call the next witness for you, so it may be a little bit out of order.

This case is about greed. It's about a man who was no longer employed, no longer had a source of income, and is greedy—and, he wishes to receive drug proceeds. You will hear about that case—you will hear the evidence, you will see the video, you will see the phone tolls. You will see the photographs. At the end of the case, we will ask you to return a verdict that is just, fair, and will speak the truth.

MR. CLARK: May it please the court, Ladies and

Gentlemen. Good afternoon. This is my opportunity to tell you what I expect the evidence is going to be. But, remember—they weren't there, she wasn't there, you weren't there. What we are telling you is kind of like a road map—if you were going from here to California, you wouldn't jump in your car and take off. You would get a road map to see where you're going. But, the fact you look at a road map doesn't mean you've seen the scenery. You don't see the scenery until you drive down the highway—and, that's going to be like this trial.

All the information you're going to have to make your decision is going to come from that witness stand. Either from live witnesses, or from documents. So, wait to determine what someone said—or, didn't say. Or, what the evidence is until you hear the live witnesses. Don't believe the road map—believe the live witnesses.

Now, we believe, in this case, the government has the burden of proof. They have the highest burden in jurisprudence—proof beyond a reasonable doubt. That's their burden. And, the reason they have that burden—and the reason they go first—is because of the burden. They have to prove beyond a reasonable doubt.

They get to call their witnesses first, and they get to examine their witnesses and determine what they say. Don't decide what a witness has or has not said until you hear the direct examination and my cross examination. It's like—can all of you see my hand? Can everybody see my hand? No, you can see this side of my hand, but you can't see my hand until I turn it around. And, like my daddy always said, "Regardless of how thin you make a pancake, there's two sides to every one of them." There will be two sides to this—trust me, there will be two sides to this story.

At the same time, the judge already told you Sherman

comes in this courtroom presumed, by you, to be innocent. That should be in your mind, so, when you hear evidence, you can determine for yourself with that presumption of innocence what the evidence means.

Now—we think and we believe the evidence in this case is going to show you Sherman Williams was a high school football player here in Mobile, and went on to the University of Alabama. He was an outstanding college athlete at the University of Alabama and, when he got out of Alabama, he was drafted by the Dallas Cowboys. The Cowboys paid him two million dollars to play football for them over a four-year period—'95, '96, '97 and '98 was the period of the two million dollars. He got a six hundred thousand dollar bonus, up front, that he put in the bank. I think the evidence is going to show you he made in excess of two to three hundred thousand dollars a year from 1995 through 1998.

In 1999, he came down here and signed with the Mobile Admirals, and he played football that summer. He was supposed to have been paid, I believe, eighty thousand dollars, so he wasn't unemployed. Then Dallas picked him back up in September of 1999 and, by the league regulations, they had to pay him a minimum salary of three hundred and seventy-five thousand dollars. That's divided over the whole season. The number of games. So, at no time was Sherman Williams unemployed, and we believe the evidence will show you to the contrary.

In addition, we believe the evidence is going to show you while Sherman was in Texas, he was single and he met a lot of people out there. And, as we all know, when you're a high-priced, high-paid athlete, there are going to be people hanging on saying, "I'm his friend, I'm his friend. That sort of thing . . ."

We expect the evidence to show you—could we have the

board back up? I'm sorry. We think the evidence is going to show you while Sherman was out in Texas, he met a lady by the name of Demetric Beans, and that she is going to tell you she had all the contacts for the marijuana—that's what she's going to say.

We expect the evidence to show you while Sherman was out in Texas playing football, his life-long friends, Frank Freeman and Roderick Ward—with whom he went to school—went to Texas on a few occasions to watch games and party—that sort of thing. While they were out there, we expect the evidence to show you they met Demetric Beans. And we expect the evidence to show you Roderick Ward had been in prison for some time for his drug dealings. Roderick Ward met Demetric Beans, and they struck up an agreement to distribute certain drugs. We also expect the evidence to show you Frank Freeman was with Roderick Ward when they went to Texas to pick up the drugs.

We expect the evidence to show you Mr. Sanders is deceased, but Demetrius Thomas was also part of that organization. We expect the evidence to show you once these people were apprehended, that's the time they said somebody else did it. We believe the evidence is going to show you who had the source, who was making trips out to Texas, and what they were doing. And, we expect the evidence to show you Sherman Williams was not the one setting up these deals. It was Beans, Freeman, Ward, and Thomas who were setting these up. We expect the evidence to show you each and every one of these people received something from the government for their testimony. We expect the evidence to show you they are being given their freedom for their testimony here today. We expect the evidence to further show you Beans, Freeman, and Ward are liars. They admit to being liars.

Mr. Freeman plead guilty to being a liar, and we expect the evidence to show you they made numerous promises, none of which they fulfilled. Yet, the government is relying on these liars in their case. We ask you to consider these people. When you see them on the witness stand, we ask you to look them in the eye and make your own determination as to whether or not you think they're telling the truth about these issues.

Now—it wasn't until April of this year that anybody ever mentioned Sherman Williams. It wasn't until this trial they said he was unemployed, and we believe the evidence is going to be to the contrary. Sherman Williams had nothing to do with Demetric Beans, Freeman, and Ward or their drug dealings. And, he had plenty of money. In fact, we expect the evidence is going to show you at this time he had almost eight hundred thousand dollars in a bank account—which is contrary to his being broke, having to do something illegal to make money.

We think after you hear all the evidence and you see all the witnesses, you will have no alternative but to find Sherman Williams not guilty.

Thank you.

THE COURT: Alright. Ms. Griffin, call your first witness.

MS. GRIFFIN: We call Frank Freeman.

THE COURT: Mr. Freeman, if you will come on up here, please, Sir. Just stand right over here by the court reporter. Thank you—that's fine.

The witness, after having first been duly sworn to tell the truth, the whole truth, and nothing but the truth, was examined and testified as follows:

DIRECT EXAMINATION BY MS. GRIFFIN:

Q: Tell us your name, please, Sir.

A: Frank Freeman.

Q: Mr. Freeman, how old are you?

A: Twenty-eight.

Q: Where do you live?

A: Minneapolis.

Q: Where did you live before you moved to Minneapolis?

A: Wolf Ridge Road, Apartment 19.

Q: Was that in Mobile?

A: Yes—that's in Whistler.

Q: Mr. Freeman, have you plead guilty to conspiracy to possess with intent to distribute marijuana?

A: Yes, Ma'am.

Q: Have you also plead guilty to theft of government property?

A: Yes, Ma'am.

Q: Now, Mr. Freeman, after you plead to these charges, you were released on bond. Is that correct?

A: Yes, Ma'am.

Q: And, have you violated one of the terms of your release?

A: Yes, Ma'am.

Q: Has the United States filed a motion to revoke your release?

A: Yes, Ma'am.

Q: Mr. Freeman, as part of your plea agreement, did you agree to attempt to provide substantial assistance to the United States?

A: Yes, Ma'am.

Q: What did you agree to do?

A: Give them the witness—I gave them the man they wanted. You know, who was connected with the marijuana.

Q: Who first gave his name to law enforcement?

A: I did.

Q: Now, Mr. Freeman, do you hope to receive a lighter sentence because of your cooperation?

A: Yes, Ma'am.

Q: Do you understand that is entirely up to the judge?

A: Yes, Ma'am.

Q: And, do you understand if you provide substantial assistance, the United States will ask the court to consider it?

A: Yes, Ma'am.

Q: Have you been promised any specific sentence?

A: No, Ma'am.

Q: Do you understand who decides what sentence you

receive?

A: Yes, Ma'am.

Q: Who is that?

A: The judge.

Q: And, you plead guilty to two felonies, and you're awaiting sentencing?

A: Yes.

Q: Mr. Freeman, do you know Sherman Williams?

A: Yes, Ma'am.

Q: How do you know him?

A: We were schoolmates since the second grade.

Q: Where was that? What city?

A: Prichard.

Q: So, you have known him then how many years?

A: Like . . .

Q: Twenty-two?

A: Twenty-two years.

Q: Since the second grade?

A: Yes, Ma'am.

Q: He is also . . . is Mr. Williams also twenty-eight?

A: No, Ma'am. He's twenty-seven.

Q: He was a year behind you?

A: Yes, Ma'am.

Q: Do you see him in the courtroom today?

A: Yes, Ma'am.

Q: Could you point him out for us?

A: (Witness complies)

Q: Can you tell me what he's wearing?

A: A blue jacket, blue shirt.

MS. GRIFFIN: Let the record reflect he identified the Defendant.

Q: Mr. Freeman, I want to direct your attention to April of 2000. Did Sherman Williams have any facial hair then?

A: A little bit.

Q: Around his mouth, sort of a goatee type thing?

A: Similar to mine.

Q: Pardon me?

A: Similar to mine.

Q: Around the side of his mouth?

A: Yes, Ma'am.

Q: Mr. Williams—excuse me, Mr. Freeman—in the course of your association with Sherman, did you ever work for Sherman Williams?

A: Yes, Ma'am.

Q: Pardon?

A: Yes, Ma'am.

Q: What type of work did you do for him?

A: Transporting marijuana from Texas to Mobile.

Q: When did you begin transporting the marijuana for Sherman Williams?

A: Around '97.

Q: How did that begin?

A: I was in a struggle. I need to pay my bills. I got behind. So, I asked him for some help, and that's what he referred.

Q: You asked who for some help?

A: Sherman Williams for some help.

Q: What did he say you could do?

A: Take a ride to Dallas—you know, pick up some marijuana, and come back to Mobile with it.

Q: How was Sherman Williams employed the in '97 and '98?

A: A football player for the Cowboys.

Q: That was in Dallas, Texas?

A: Yes, Ma'am.

Q: And, did you agree to do that? Transport for Sherman Williams?

A: Yes, Ma'am.

Q: What did you receive for transporting marijuana for Sherman Williams?

A: Some financial help.

Q: You hoped to receive some money?

A: Yes, Ma'am.

Q: Mr. Freeman, did there come a time when you were transporting marijuana for Sherman Williams, and you were arrested?

A: Yes, Ma'am.

Q: When was that?

A: The 19th—18th.

Q: Was it the 20th of 2000?

A: Yes, Ma'am.

Q: Where were you arrested?

A: In Tyler, Texas.

Q: Where is that?

A: Coming from Dallas, Texas.

Q: Toward Mobile?

A: Yes, Ma'am.

Q: So, it's east of Dallas?

A: Yes, Ma'am.

Q: Who arrested you?

A: A trooper from Texas.

Q: A Texas trooper. What car were you in?

A: Volkswagon Jetta.

Q: Where did you get that vehicle?

A: From a car lot on Highway 90.

Q: And, how is it you got that vehicle?

A: Sherman.

Q: When you say Highway 90, you mean in Mobile?

A: Yes, Ma'am.

Q: How was it that you got the vehicle?

A: Well, Sherman went to pay the repossession fee on it, and he asked me to ride with him to pick it up.

Q: So, did you ride with Sherman to Highway 90 to pick up the Volkswagon Jetta?

A: Yes, Ma'am.

Q: Who else was with you?

A: Mark Mixon.

Q: What happened when you and Sherman got to the car dealership?

A: Sherman and I got out, he walked in, and proceeded to pay the man for the rest of the repossession money. Then he got the car out of the garage where he had it.

Q: Did you receive the Volkswagon Jetta from Sherman Williams?

A: Yes, Ma'am.

MS. GRIFFIN: Your Honor, may I approach the witness?

THE COURT: Any time you have an exhibit, just come up. You don't have to ask.

MS. GRIFFIN:

Q: I show you what's marked as Government's Exhibit 1, and ask you if you can identify the exhibit?

A: Yes, Ma'am.

Q: What is that a photograph of?

A: A Volkswagon Jetta.

Q: That's the Jetta Sherman Williams gave you to use?

A: Yes, Ma'am.

MS. GRIFFIN: I move to admit Government's Exhibit 1.

MR . CLARK: No objection.

THE COURT: Mark it in.

MS. GRIFFIN: Your Honor, can we publish it to the jury?

THE COURT: Alright.

MS. GRIFFIN:

Q: Mr. Freeman, this is the car in which you were arrested in Texas?

A: Yes, Ma'am.

Q: Okay. So, you told us you got this car in Mobile on Highway 90. How did you get to Texas?

A: We drove from Mobile to Texas in that car.

Q: Who did?

A: Sherman, Mark, and I.

Q: Mark who?

A: Mixon.

Q: How soon after you got it from the car lot did you, Sherman Williams, and Mark Mixon drive to Texas in the Volkswagon Jetta?

A: I would say like about thirty, or forty-five minutes.

Q: What happened when you got to Texas? Excuse me, I want to back up. You left Mobile?

A: Yes, Ma'am.

Q: You, Mark Mixon, and Sherman Williams?

A: Yes, Ma'am.

Q: Did you make any stops before you got to Texas?

A: Yes, Ma'am.

Q: Where was that?

A: We stopped at a Hardy's and ate for a minute, as well as Hattiesburg, Mississippi.

Q: Alright. And, did you stop anywhere in Jackson, Mississippi?

A: Yes, Ma'am—at a Fairfield Inn.

Q: Is that a hotel?

A: Yes, Ma'am.

Q: Who stopped at the Fairfield Inn?

A: Me, Sherman, and Mark.

Q: And, what happened when you, Sherman, and Mark Mixon got to the Fairfield Inn?

A: We met a gentleman there—last name Rice.

THE COURT: What was the last name?

THE WITNESS: Rice.

THE COURT: Wright—W-R-I-G-H-T?

THE WITNESS: R-I-C-E.

THE COURT: Oh . . . Rice.

MS. GRIFFIN:

Q: Where was Mr. Rice?

A: He drove up on the side of us. Sherman called him on the phone to let him know we were there.

Q: Sherman Williams called who?

A: Rice. On the phone . . .

Q: Did Sherman Williams have a cellular telephone?

A: Yes, Ma'am.

Q: So, once you got to Jackson, Mississippi, Sherman

Williams called Mr. Rice?

A: Yes, Ma'am.

Q: And, did you hear Sherman Williams's end of that telephone conversation?

A: Excuse me?

Q: I asked, did you hear Sherman Williams's end of the telephone conversation?

A: No, Ma'am. I really wasn't paying attention to his conversation.

Q: After the conversation, where did you and Sherman Williams go?

A: We waited at Burger King for a minute, and the guy pulled up, and we followed him to the Fairfield Inn. Sherman, Rice, and I walked into the Fairfield Inn.

Q: One person pulled up?

A: Yes, Ma'am.

Q: I show you what's marked as Government's Exhibit 4, and ask if you can identify the photograph.

A: Yes, Ma'am.

Q: Who is that a picture of?

A: Mr. Rice.

Q: The same individual you saw at the Fairfield Inn?

A: Yes, Ma'am.

MS . GRIFFIN: We move to admit the government's Exhibit 4.

CLARK: No objection.

THE COURT: Mark it in.

MS. GRIFFIN:

Q: Mr. Freeman, why were you, Mr. Williams, and Mr. Mixon going to Texas?

A: To pick up some marijuana.

Q: And, why did you and Mr. Williams stop to meet with Kenneth Rice?

A: Because Mr. Rice was supposed to pick up a package also—some marijuana also, or some cocaine or something. But, I didn't find out until later it was suppose to have been some cocaine he was suppose to receive.

Q: Now, when you got to the Fairfield Inn, who went inside the Fairfield Inn?

A: Sherman Williams and I.

Q: And, who was in the room with you and Sherman Williams?

A: Mr. Rice.

Q: What occurred in the Fairfield Inn room?

A: We went inside the room, and proceeded to start to count some money. And, I was sitting down in the chair where he was counting the money for a minute.

Q: What type of room was it in the Fairfield Inn?

A: It was one bed in there. You know—like a nice little

suite.

Q: Did it appear to be a special type of room?

A: No, Ma'am. It was nothing fancy.

Q: Was it a handicapped room?

A: I don 't think so.

Q: Now, Mr. Freeman . . .

A: Yes, Ma'am?

Q: Who was counting the money?

A: Sherman and Rice.

Q: Who had the money?

A: Both of them.

Q: No—who first had the money?

A: Rice.

Q: And, what was it contained in?

A: Bags. It was in little bags.

Q: Did you watch Sherman Williams and Mr. Rice count the money?

A: Yes, Ma'am.

Q: How much money was it?

A: It got up to like about thirty-four and thirty-eight thousand. Between there.

Q: It was cash—United States currency?

A: Yes, Ma'am.

Q: What happened to that money?

A: Rice gave me twelve hundred to put in my pocket for me, and the rest of it they put in Ziplock bags.

Q: Who put it in Ziplock bags?

A: Sherman and Rice put it in Ziplock bags.

Q: And, what conversation did you overhear between Kenneth Rice and Sherman Williams about the money?

A: We was just suppose to bring this package back, and when we get back, give him a call.

Q: Who was supposed to bring whose package back?

A: I was suppose to bring Rice's package back. When I got back, I was supposed to give him a call. When I got into Jackson . . .

Q: What was Rice purchasing from Sherman?

A: As the trip went on, I found out that it was suppose to have been . . .

MR. CLARK: Judge, I object to how he found out.

THE COURT: Restate your question, Ms. Griffin.

MS. GRIFFIN:

Q: Did there come a time when you learned what Sherman was purchasing for Kenneth Rice?

A: Yes, Ma'am.

Q: How did you learn that?

A: Sherman told me he was suppose to pick up some cocaine for Kenneth Rice.

Q: What quantity?

A: Probably about two keys.

MR . CLARK: Judge, I object to 'probably' . . .

THE COURT: Well, that's cross examination. Overruled. That's cross.

MS. GRIFFIN:

Q: Who told you that?

A: Sherman.

Q: Now, Mr. Freeman—in the hotel where you said there was thirty-four to thirty-eight thousand dollars of currency, who had the money?

A: Sherman and Rice.

Q: Alright. Who left the room with the money?

A: Sherman and I.

Q: Who had the larger share of the money? You said you had one thousand two hundred dollars in your pocket.

A: Yes, Ma'am. Then he gave me some more in a bag to go put in a black bag in the car.

Q: Who did?

A: Sherman gave me some more.

Q: And, you put it in what?

A: In a black bag.

Q: Who directed you to do that?

A: Sherman did.

Q: I show you what's marked as Government's Exhibit 5, and ask you if you can identify the bag.

A: Yes, Ma'am.

Q: Is this the bag you put the United States currency in?

A: Yes, Ma'am.

Q: Mr. Freeman, after you and Sherman Williams got back in the Jetta to go back to Texas, where was the money?

A: It was in the bag.

Q: The black bag you identified?

 A: Yes, Ma'am.

Q: Where was Mr. Rice when you and Mr. Williams left?

A: He jumped back in his vehicle, and he left.

Q: What type of vehicle was he in?

A: A silver Expedition.

Q: Now, Mr. Freeman, I want to show you Government's Exhibit 3, and ask you if you can identify it.

A: Yes, Ma'am.

Q: Is that a hotel record for the Fairfield Inn in Pearl,

Mississippi?

A: Yes, Ma'am.

Q: At the Fairfield Inn, Jacksonville Airport?

A: Yes, Ma'am.

MS. GRIFFIN: Your Honor, these were subpoenaed from the Fairfield Inn.

MR. CLARK: No objection.

MS. GRIFFIN: And, a custodian would show this is Kenneth Rice's registration, Fairfield Inn, April 19 and 20 of 2000.

Q: I show you Government's Exhibit 3 (b), and ask if you can identify the photograph.

A: Yes, Ma'am.

Q: What is that a photograph of?

A: Burger King.

Q: Was this a Burger King where you stopped?

A: Yes, Ma'am.

Q: I will show you the inside. If you will, tell us what that's a photograph of.

A: The Fairfield Inn.

Q: Is that where you stopped?

A: Yes, Ma'am.

Q: Can you see the Fairfield Inn from the Burger King?

A: Yes, Ma'am.

Q: Does that picture depict it?

A: Yes, Ma'am.

Q: And, that's Jackson, Mississippi?

A: Yes, Ma'am.

Q: So, Mr. Freeman, Mr. Mixon did not come into the Fairfield Inn?

A: No, Ma'am.

Q: When you and Sherman got back in the car with the money in the black case, where did you go?

A: We proceeded to head to Texas.

Q: How did you get there?

A: In the Volkswagon Jetta.

Q: What route did you take?

A: Interstate 20.

Q: Mr. Freeman, you went from Mobile, to Hattiesburg, to Jackson, Mississippi?

A: Yes, Ma'am.

Q: And, then you went straight toward Fort Worth and Dallas, is that right?

A: Yes, Ma'am.

Q: Does that depict the route you took, I-20?

A: Yes, Ma'am.

Q: These are the cities you passed through—Monroe, Shreveport, and Tyler?

A: Yes, Ma'am.

Q: Now, did Sherman Williams still have his cell phone while you were going that route?

A: Yes, Ma'am.

Q: Was he using it on occasion?

A: Occasionally.

Q: Mr. Freeman, what did you do when you got to the Dallas-Fort Worth area?

A: We went to this guy's house when we first got there.

MR. CLARK: Judge, I'm having difficulty hearing him.

MS. GRIFFIN:

Q: You'll have to speak up.

A: We went to this guy's house named T when we first got there.

Q: Where was that?

A: In Fort Worth, Texas.

Q: Had you ever seen T before?

A: No Ma'am.

Q: Who introduced you to T?

A: Sherman did.

Q: What happened?

A: We sat there for a little bit—you know, talked a little

bit, went and got a bag of marijuana, smoked, then we went to a Ramada Limited and got a couple of rooms.

Q: Who got a couple of rooms?

A: Sherman and I.

Q: When you say you smoked, what did you mean?

A: Marijuana.

Q: You, Sherman, and T?

A: Yes.

Q: Who provided the marijuana?

A: T.

Q: Mr. Freeman, who checked in at the Ramada Limited?

A: I did.

Q: Who went with you to the hotel?

A: Sherman.

MS. GRIFFIN:

Q: I show you what's marked as Government's Exhibit 6, and ask if you can identify the hotel documents.

A: Yes, Ma'am.

Q: What are those, please, Sir?

A: For the room, receipts.

Q: That's where you checked in?

A: Yes, Ma'am.

Q: And, these are the documents showing where you signed in?

A: Yes, Ma'am.

Q: From the hotel, is that correct?

A: Yes, Ma'am.

Q: Does it show you signing on April 19th of 2000?

A: Yes, Ma'am.

Q: And, does it show you getting two separate rooms?

A: Yes, Ma'am.

Q: Is that your signature—Frank J. Freeman?

A: Yes, Ma'am.

Q: Why did you get two rooms?

A: Because Sherman wanted his own individual room, and me and Mark had to have a room.

Q: Who paid for the rooms?

A: Sherman did.

Q: Mr. Freeman, what did you do the following day, the 20th?

A: I got a call from Sherman, and he told me to come to his room. He gave me some money, and he told me to keep it.

Q: How much money did he give you?

A: Twenty thousand.

Q: Was it in currency?

A: Yes, Ma'am.

Q: What were you to do when you met T?

A: I was supposed to go pick up fifty pounds of weed—marijuana—and head back toward the hotel after we picked it up.

Q: Did you meet T?

A: Yes, Ma'am.

Q: Where did that take place?

A: We went back to T's house.

Q: What happened there?

A: Parked the Jetta, the Volkswagon, got in the car with him, he went to a distinctive area, and met with some people.

Q: I can't hear you now.

A: We went to a distinctive area, and met with some people.

Q: He being T?

A: Yes, Ma'am.

Q: How do you know that?

A: I was with him.

Q: Alright. And what did you see happen?

A: He asked me to give him the money before we got out of the Jeep. I gave him the money, and I walked in with him to purchase the marijuana. We counted the bags—individually wrapped bags, you know. Twenty-five in each garbage bag. We weighed them, weighed them up, and then we walked out.

Q: Who walked out.

A: T and I.

Q: How many bags were there in all?

A: Fifty.

Q: Packaged individually? One pound each?

A: Yes, Ma'am.

Q: Twenty-five in one bag, and twenty-five in the other?

A: Yes, Ma'am.

Q: What type of bags were they in?

A: Ziplock freezer bags.

Q: Within the Ziplock freezer bags in a black garbage bag?

A: Yes, Ma'am.

Q: From whom did you receive the marijuana?

A: From some Mexicans.

Q: What did you do with the marijuana?

A: Put it in the Jeep, and we left.

Q: So, it was fifty pounds of marijuana?

A: Yes, Ma'am.

Q: After you got the marijuana, what did you do?

A: We went back to T 's house, and put it in the Jetta.

Q: Wait just a minute—before you get to going to T's house, who gave you the money to pay for the marijuana?

A: Sherman did.

Q: Whose marijuana was it?

A: Sherman's.

Q: Did you take it to Dee's house?

A: To Dee's house?

Q: Dee's house.

A: Yes, we did.

Q: At whose direction?

A: Sherman's.

Q: Who is Dee?

A: One of his lady friends.

Q: I show you what's marked as Government's Exhibit 7, and ask if you can identify the photograph?

A: Yes, Ma'am.

Q: Who is that a photograph of?

A: Sherman, Dee, and me.

Q: That's a picture of you, Dee, and Sherman together?

A: Yes, Ma'am.

Q: Then a photograph of Dee—is that correct?

A: Yes, Ma'am.

Q: Is Dee the lady whose house you went to?

A: Yes, Ma'am.

Q: Mr. Freeman, where does Dee live?

A: In Texas—in Dallas.

Q: Where was her apartment?

A: Somewhere out there in Texas.

Q: Had you been to her apartment before?

A: Yes, Ma'am.

Q: Had you been to her apartment before with Sherman Williams?

A: Yes, Ma'am.

Q: I ask if you can identify the photograph?

A: Yes, Ma'am.

Q: What is that a picture of?

A: Dee's apartment.

Q: In what city?

A: In Texas—in Dallas, Texas.

Q: Mr. Freeman, before I publish Exhibit 8, look at Exhibit 7 on the screen. That shows Demetric Beans, Sherman Williams, and you—is that right?

A: Yes, Ma'am.

Q: Where was that picture taken?

A: We was at a club somewhere in Mobile.

Q: That was before, obviously, your stop in Texas?

A: Yes, Ma'am.

Q: Once you got to Dee's house in Texas with the fifty pounds of marijuana, what did you do?

A: We parked the car up under the shed, walked into the house, and sat down for a minute.

Q: Who was with you?

A: Me, Sherman, and Mark Mixon.

Q: Now, did Sherman come there by himself?

A: To Dee's house?

Q: Yes.

A: No, Ma'am.

Q: How did he get there?

A: He was with us in the Jetta.

Q: He was in the Jetta with you when you picked up the marijuana from T?

A: No, Ma'am.

Q: Okay. Explain to us how you got him with you.

A: After I picked up the marijuana from T, I went back to the hotel, and picked him up from the Ramada Limited.

Q: You picked Sherman Williams up from the Ramada Limited?

A: Yes, Ma'am.

Q: Where was the marijuana?

A: It was still in the trunk of the car.

Q: Where did you go?

A: Then we went to Dee's house.

Q: What happened at Dee's house?

A: We sat and waited. And, at that time, you know, I asked him what we was waiting on.

Q: Asked who?

A: I asked Sherman what we was waiting on. He told me he was supposed to be getting two keys for Rice. I said, "Didn't nobody tell me nothing about no cocaine—you're going to have to pay me more.

Q: What did he tell you?

A: I'm going to have to talk to Rice about that.

Q: Who said that?

A: Sherman said I had to talk to a Rice about that.

Q: Did Sherman Williams use a cellular telephone?

A: I didn't see him because he didn't use the phone then. I think he probably used the house phone. I don't have no idea.

Q: Do you know whether he tried to talk to Kenneth Rice?

A: No Ma'am.

Q: Did you . . . were you and Sherman Williams able to purchase the two kilograms of cocaine?

A: No, Ma'am.

Q: What happened to forbid you from doing that?

A: Well, the deal just didn't go through. And, you know, Mark and I, we left for a minute. We walked and got something to eat, you know, while we was eating. And, after that, we came back and I was ready to go. You know, I already had been away from home already too long, so I was ready to go.

Q: Did Sherman tell you anything else at Dee's s house about the two kilograms of cocaine?

A: No, Ma'am.

Q: Did you and Mr. Mixon leave Dee's apartment?

A: Yes, Ma'am.

Q: Where were you headed?

A: We was headed back to Mobile.

Q: Where was the marijuana when you left?

A: Still in the trunk of the car.

Q: And, that was the Jetta?

A: Yes, Ma'am.

Q: Where was Sherman Williams when you left?

A: Still at Dee's.

Q: What instructions were you given?

A: He gave me directions to get back—the way to get back to I-20 to head back toward Mobile.

Q: Who gave you those?

A: Sherman gave me directions to get back to I-20.

Q: What were you to do with the marijuana?

A: Bring it to my house, and wait until he got there.

Q: Wait until who got there?

A: Wait until Sherman got there.

Q: To Mobile?

A: Yes, Ma'am.

Q: Who told you that?

A: Sherman told me that.

Q: Mr. Freeman, did you leave to come to Mobile?

A: Yes, Ma'am.

Q: What happened to you once you left the apartment with the marijuana headed to Mobile?

A: We got pulled over in Tyler, Texas.

Q: Tyler, Texas is just a little bit out from Dallas and Fort Worth on the way to Mobile on I-20?

A: Yes, Ma'am.

Q: What did you get pulled over for?

A: Said I was riding in two lanes.

Q: Were you driving?

A: Yes, Ma'am.

Q: What happened when you were stopped?

A: He walked up to the car, said he smelled marijuana, and he asked me if he could search the car.

Q: Did you offer to tell him he could search?

A: At first I told him no, and he told me he would make me wait there until he bring the dog. Me knowing the fact that it's already there, ain't no need to bring no dog.

Q; You knew the dog would find it?

A: Yes, Ma'am.

Q: So, you did tell them they could go ahead and search your vehicle?

A: Yes, Ma'am.

Q: Did you tell him anything about Sherman Williams during that stop?

A: They was constantly asking me who was Shake 20, who was Shake 20, who was Roderick Ward. I come to find out the car was in Roderick Ward's name. I don't get down like that. I didn't know that.

Q: You didn't know the Jetta was in Roderick Ward's name at that time, did you?

A: No, Ma'am.

Q: Did you know Roderick Ward?

A: Yes, Ma'am.

Q: Who was Roderick Ward?

A: One of his friends.

Q: One of whose friends?

A: One of Sherman's friends. He was suppose to be a runner like I was—I was supposed to be a runner.

Q: You knew Roderick Ward to be a runner for Sherman Williams, as well?

A: Yes, Ma'am.

Q: Mr. Freeman, what was found in the Volkswagon Jetta?

A: Fifty pounds of marijuana.

Q: Were you arrested?

A: Yes. Ma'am, I was.

Q: Did you tell the officers what you were doing and who you were doing it for?

A: Yes. Ma'am, I did.

Q: Based on that, did you agree to attempt a controlled delivery to Sherman Williams?

A: Yes, I did.

Q: After you agreed to cooperate, what happened?

A: They drove me to Jackson, Mississippi. The troopers from Texas drove me to Jackson,Mississippi, and met with the DEA agents from Mobile. And, the DEA agents from Mobile drove me to Mobile.

Q: Where was the marijuana on your way to Mobile from the stop in Tyler, Texas?

A: It was still in the trunk of the Jetta.

Q: When you arrived in Jackson, Mississippi—you, the Jetta, and the marijuana were turned over to agents from

Mobile?

A: Yes, Ma'am.

Q: Where did you go from there?

A: From Jackson, Mississippi, to Mobile.

Q: In Mobile, did you tell the officer what you were to do with the marijuana?

A: Yes, Ma'am.

Q: Based on that, what did you agree to do?

A: They asked me to wear a wire, and set up a surveillance camera in my apartment.

Q: Did you agree to do that?

A: Yes, Ma'am.

Q: Where was your apartment, Mr. Freeman? I show you what's marked as Government's Exhibit 9, and ask if you can identify the photographs.

A: Yes, Ma'am.

Q: Can you tell us what these are photographs of, Mr. Freeman?

A: Of the apartment complex where I was currently staying.

Q: That's the apartment complex where you were living?

A: Yes, Ma'am.

Q: And, on the back, does that show the stairs near your apartment?

A: Yes, Ma'am.

Q: Was your apartment upstairs or downstairs?

A: Downstairs.

Q: Mr. Freeman, in publishing the exhibit to the jury, at the top is the picture on the bottom left-hand corner your apartment?

THE COURT: You said the picture on the bottom. You mean the window?

MS. GRIFFIN:

Q: Excuse me, the window. Is this your apartment here?

A: Yes, Ma'am.

Q: Down at the bottom. And, the stairs go up to the next level?

A: Yes, Ma'am.

Q: What is around the back of your apartment?

A: A big field and ditches.

Q: I show you Government's Exhibit 9 (b), and ask if you can identify the chart.

A: Yes, Ma'am.

Q: What is that a chart of?

A. The apartment complex where I lived.

Q: Does it identify your apartment?

A: Yes, Ma'am.

Q: Mr. Freeman, could you step down to show us Wolf Ridge Road and your apartment?

A: Right here.

Q: Point, so they can see it.

A: Going to the apartment, my apartment is right here on the corner.

Q: There are woods behind your apartment, is that correct?

A: Yes, Ma'am.

Q: Did the officers set up video equipment in your apartment?

A: Yes. Ma'am, they did.

Q: Audio and video?

A: Yes, Ma'am.

Q: Mr. Freeman, did you have a telephone there at the apartment?

A: Yes. Ma'am, I did.

Q: Can you tell us that number?

A: 330-0876

Q: That 's area code—334?

A: Yes, Ma'am.

Q: Whose name was the phone in?

A: In Katrina Washington's name.

Q: That was your wife, is that right?

A: Yes, Ma'am.

Q: 330—0876. What had the previous number been?

A: 330-0047.

MR . CLARK: I'm sorry, I didn't get that.

THE WITNESS: 330-0047.

MS. GRIFFIN:

Q: Now, Mr. Freeman, after it was wired, approximately what time was it when the wiring was completed?

A: It was completed early that morning.

Q: By then, was it the morning of the 21st of April?

A: Yes, Ma'am.

Q: Where was the marijuana during this time?

A: In a dining area on the floor.

Q: Who was there with you at the apartment with the marijuana?

A: The DEA agents.

Q: Was Ms. Ridenour there with the FBI?

A: Yes, Ma'am.

Q: And, Mr. Fagan?

A: Yes, Ma'am.

Q: Did you make some phone calls that morning?

A: Yes, Ma'am.

Q: Who did you call?

A: Sherman Williams.

Q: Why were you doing that?

A: To let him know I was there.

Q: Did you consent to recording those calls?

A: Yes, Ma'am.

Q: They were recorded?

A: Yes, Ma'am.

Q: Were you able to speak with Sherman Williams?

A: Yes, Ma'am.

Q: In fact, did you tape three conversations with him?

A: Yes, Ma'am.

Q: And, where was Sherman Williams when you were calling? Where did you call?

A: I called Dee's apartment.

Q: In what city?

A: Dallas, Texas.

Q: Now, I show you Government's Exhibit 10 (a). Have you previously listened to the tapes of those telephone conversations?

A: Yes, Ma'am.

Q: I will show you Government's Exhibit 10 (a), (c), and (d). Have you read the transcripts of the telephone conversations?

A: Yes, Ma'am.

Q: Have you compared the transcripts with the tapes of the calls?

A. Yes, Ma'am.

A: Did you have three telephone calls with Sherman Williams that you recorded the morning of April 21st of 2000?

Q: Yes, Ma'am.

MS GRIFFIN: Your Honor, we move to admit the tape, Exhibit 10 (a), and to use the transcripts as aids to the jury when we play the tape.

MR. CLARK: No objection, Your Honor.

THE COURT: Alright. Mark those in. Now, Ladies and Gentlemen, let me explain to you what we are about to do. In a moment, somebody will tell you how to put these headsets on. I could probably do it, but I will let them show you how to turn it on so you can listen to the tape recording of the conversation the witness has testified about. The other exhibit is a transcript typed out of the spoken word—this witness says he has read it, and said it's what's here on the tape. If there is any difference in what you hear with your ears and what you see someone typed on the transcript, it is what you hear that is the evidence, Not the transcript. The transcript is given to you as an aid to recognize and hear words that—because they are not familiar in the sense of whose voices they are, the tone, or connection—you might not otherwise understand what this witness is saying. These words on e-paper is what he heard with his ear. That's for you to decide, if that's what s on the tape.

MS GRIFFIN:

Q: Mr. Freeman, why were you calling Mr. Williams on the 21st?

A: To let him know I was at home and, also, the agents wanted him to get to Mobile for him to pick up those packages.

Q: Were you trying to find out when he would arrive in Mobile?

A: Yes, Ma'am.

Q: Your Honor, we will publish the transcripts.

THE COURT: Now, are you going to do one at a time, Ms. Griffin? Were these calls . . .

MS. GRIFFIN: Yes, Sir. I would like to do one, two, three. They were in fairly quick succession—then I will pass the second one out. They are very short.

THE COURT: So, you will pass the first transcript out first.

MS. GRIFFIN: The first one.

THE COURT: Okay. That's 10 what—(b)?

MS. GRIFFIN: 10(b).

THE COURT: Pass that out. Ladies and Gentlemen, do not read it. Just put it in your lap because we don't want you to read it until you hear the audio. Again, let me explain. You don't t have to read this transcript. This is given to you as an aid. You're welcome to read it—you might find it helpful as you listen. But, again, as you hear it, that's what the evidence is.

MS. GRIFFIN: Ms. Ridenour will explain to you how to use the headsets you have in your chair.

(Tape played in open court)

MS. GRIFFIN: Okay, Mr. Freeman, did you tell Sherman Williams about the trip?

A: Yes, Ma'am.

Q: You made some reference to, "No, I ain't took nothing out of it." What did he ask you?

A: Did I take any marijuana out of the bag.

Q: Did you determine what time you thought he was coming?

A: Yes, Ma'am.

Q: And, did you determine whether he was coming to your apartment or not?

A: Yes, Ma'am.

Q: After this call, did you make a second call to Sherman Williams?

A: Yes, Ma'am.

Q: Mr. Freeman, were you attempting to find out if Sherman Williams were going to pick up the marijuana?

A: Yes, Ma'am.

Q: Who was that?

A: Somebody was suppose to have went in on it with him.

Q: So, during the conversation, he says he gave you one thousand, two hundred dollars. Did you receive one thousand, two hundred dollars?

A: Not from him.

Q: Who did you receive it from?

A: From Rice.

Q: So, at that time, you didn't know if Sherman Williams were coming, or if he were going to send someone else—is that correct?

A: Yes, Ma'am.

Q: And, did you place another phone call?

A: Yes, Ma'am.

MS . GRIFFIN: We will pass the transcript out. This is 10 (d).

THE COURT: Alright. Put your head sets on.

(Tape played in open court)

THE COURT: Okay. Please pass your transcripts down to the right. Ms. Griffin, are we going to hear anymore of this today?

MS. GRIFFIN: No, Sir.

Q: Mr. Freeman, you knew the approximate time you expected Sherman Williams at your apartment?

A: Yes, Ma'am.

Q: You had been placing those calls to Dallas, is that right ?

A: Yes, Ma'am.

Q: So, there was a down time when you thought he was traveling from Texas to Mobile?

A: Yes, Ma'am.

Q: Did Sherman Williams come to your apartment on April 21st of 2000?

A: Yes, Ma'am.

Q: About what time?

A: About around five-thirty or six o'clock.

Q: Late afternoon?

A: Yes, Ma'am.

Q: When he came, was it still daylight?

A: Yes, Ma'am.

Q: Did he come in the apartment?

A: Yes, Ma'am.

Q: Was he alone?

A: No, Ma'am.

Q: Who was with him?

A: Latasma, his girlfriend.

Q: Okay. Did she come into the apartment?

A: No, Ma'am—she dropped him off.

Q: She dropped him off?

A: Yes, Ma'am.

Q: Is she in the courtroom?

A: Yes, Ma'am.

Q: Can you point her out?

A: Back there with the black jacket on, and white collar.

Q: What did he have in his hand?

A: A black bag.

Q: This black bag you have identified as Government's Exhibit 5?

A: Yes, Ma'am.

Q: Where had you last seen this black bag?

A: When we was headed to Dallas.

Q: You didn't bring that bag—black bag—back in the Jetta with you, did you?

A: No, Ma'am.

Q: And, when you last saw it with Sherman Williams, what did it contain?

A: He had money in it.

Q: What did Sherman Williams do with the black bag when he got to your apartment?

A: Placed it on the floor.

Q: What happened when Sherman Williams came in your apartment? What did he do?

A: He got the bags of marijuana, started counting, and looking at it—just pretty much analyzed it.

Q: And, you say the bags of marijuana. Are those bags the bags you picked up for Sherman Williams in Dallas?

A: Yes, Ma'am.

Q: That had been transferred to the officers, and put in your apartment—is that right?

A: Yes, Ma'am.

Q: Was your meeting with Sherman Williams in your apartment videoed?

A: Yes, Ma'am.

Q: Have you seen the video?

A: Yes, Ma'am.

Q: Who is shown on the video?

A: Sherman and I.

Q: Was it made Äpri1 21st of 2000 when Sherman Williams came to your apartment?

A: Yes, Ma'am.

Q: I show you Government's Exhibit 12 (a), and ask if you can identify the video.

A: Yes, Ma'am.

Q: Is that a copy of a redaction of his stay at your apartment?

A: Yes, Ma'am.

Q: Now, about how long was he at your apartment?

A: About three or four hours.

Q: And, it's fair to say there was a good bit of conversation?

A: Yes, Ma'am.

Q: A good bit of guy talk?

A: Yes, Ma'am.

Q: Has this been redacted to just play the portions where you talked about drugs?

A: Yes, Ma'am.

Q: So, this is approximately forty minutes?

A: Yes, Ma'am.

Q: Does this accurately reflect what took part there between you and Sherman Williams, except for when you were doing some guy talk?

A: Yes, Ma'am.

Q: I show you Government's Exhibit 12 (b), and ask you if that is a transcript of this redacted video.

A: Yes, Ma'am.

Q: Have you compared the transcript with the video?

A: Yes, Ma'am.

Q: Does the transcript accurately reflect what occurs between you and Sherman Williams on the video?

A: Yes, Ma'am.

MS. GRIFFIN: Your Honor, we move to admit 12 (a), and move to use 12 (b) as an aid to the jury—and, we move to play the video.

MR CLARK: Judge, could I take the witness on . . .

THE COURT: Well, let's do this—let's take that up at the break. I will let the jury take a break, then we will deal with that issue when we come back.

(Court takes a 15 minute break)

THE COURT: Alright, Ladies and Gentlemen, we will continue now.

MS. GRIFFIN: If you would, pass the transcripts down, and we will play Government's Exhibit Number 12 (a).

THE COURT: Where do you plan to play it? Up here?

MS. GRIFFIN: Up here, and out loud. So, we don 't need to use the headsets.

THE COURT: Alright. Would it help to turn the light out?

MS. GRIFFIN: It will make it clearer.

THE COURT: Ladies and Gentlemen, we will give you an idea of how dark it gets.

A JUROR: We can't read.

THE COURT: You won't be able to read. Yeah—wait a minute. We have a problem. Turn the lights back on. We can't have it both ways. Let's see how it comes out without the lights off—if we can determine the image on the screen here. Again, it's not necessary that you use the transcript—it's just an aid. It will be hard to watch the video, and read this at the same time. Go ahead.

(Video tape played in open court)

THE COURT: Alright. Fold up your transcripts, and pass them down to the right.

MS. GRIFFIN: Mr. Freeman, what was in the black bag you could see Sherman Williams digging into?

A: The one-pound bag of marijuana.

Q: That's where the marijuana was?

A: Yes, Ma'am.

Q: Now—was there also another camera angled other than the video camera we saw?

A: Yes, Ma'am.

Q: In fact, there was a white light back in the far corner that contained another camera pointing at you and Mr. Williams?

A: Yes, Ma'am.

Q: You have also seen that video?

A: Yes, Ma'am.

Q: It shows just a different view of your faces than the one we have just seen. Is that Government's Exhibit 12 (c)?

A: Yes, Ma'am.

Q: Have you revised this, and does it show just a different angle of what we have seen, but showing your faces?

A: Yes, Ma'am.

MS. GRIFFIN: Your Honor, we move to admit 12 (c) and ask the court for us to play about five minutes of it. There is no audio on this portion—is there no sound?

A: No, Ma'am.

(Video tape played in open court)

MS. GRIFFIN: What was Sherman Williams doing on that video?

A: Counting the marijuana that was in the bag.

Q: Then what did he do with it?

A: Put it back in the bag.

Q: Did he take some from some of the bag, and later take some out of the bag?

A: Yes, Ma'am.

Q: What did he do with what he took out of the bags?

A: Put them in the other sandwich bag.

Q: Who gave him that sandwich bag?

A: I did.

Q: That's the point when you were talking about a chocolate chip cookie bag?

A: Yes, Ma'am.

Q: So, how much did he put in the sandwich bag?

A: Just pretty much something to smoke on.

Q: A small amount in each sandwich bag?

A: Yes, Ma'am.

Q: Mr. Freeman, when he left the apartment for the last time—when you heard them say Mobile police—what did he take out with him?

A: You mean Sherman Williams? The garbage bags full of marijuana.

Q: Fifty pounds?

A: Yes, Ma'am.

Q: What did you see him do with that marijuana?

A: Put it in the trunk.

Q: Of what vehicle?

A: The Volkswagon Jetta.

Q: When did you see that happen?

A: I seen the DEA and the task force come toward us. After that, nothing because I laid down on the ground.

Q: Inside your apartment?

A: No, outside. I was on the outside. I laid down.

Q: Did Sherman Williams stop when the police said stop?

A: I didn't know he was gone until I looked up, you know? Because I laid straight down. I seen the red beams coming from where they was pointing the guns. I laid down.

Q: Sherman Williams ran. He left, is that right?

A: Yes, Ma'am.

Q: Now, I want to back up. During the video, was there a time when Sherman Williams left your apartment?

A: Yes, Ma'am.

Q: What happened? Why did he leave?

A: Felt like somebody was watching him.

Q: Where did he go?

A: Into the next apartment complex's parking lot.

Q: And, where were you while he did that?

A: At first, I was outside. Then I came back in the house.

Q: Did he also go to get some rolling papers?

A: We went together to do that.

Q: He left twice during the video—left your apartment, right?

A: Yes, Ma'am.

Q: Once to look around the area. Did he suspect he saw something?

A: Yes, Ma'am.

Q: Did he tell you that?

A: Yes, Ma'am.

Q: When he went to get the rolling papers, did you go with him?

A: Yes, I did.

Q: Were y'all able to get rolling papers?

A: Well, we got blunts. We didn't get rolling papers. We got cigars.

Q: Did you and Mr. Williams smoke marijuana while he was at your apartment?

A: Yes, Ma'am.

Q: Mr. Freeman, early on, he mentioned something to you—"I don't ever remember you making no trip, and didn't get nothing . . ."

A: Yes, Ma'am.

Q: Had you made earlier trips for Sherman Williams other than this trip where you were stopped on April 20th?

A: Yes, Ma'am.

Q: How many trips did you make for Sherman Williams where you transported marijuana for him from Texas to Mobile?

A: Four.

Q: Approximately when did those trips occur?

A: Between '97 and '98 in the period—and, one time in '99. And, I didn't see him no more until . . .

Q: I can hardly hear you.

A: I said in the period from '97 and '98—then we stopped, and it didn't start again until like '99. Then he came to me in 2000.

Q: I want to talk about the trips in '97. Did anyone travel with you on those trips to Texas?

A: No, Ma'am.

Q: At whose direction did you go?

A: I went the direction he gave me.

Q: Who?

A: Sherman.

Q: Where did you go in Texas in '97.

A: I went to his house in Dallas.

Q: I show you what is marked as Government's Exhibit 13, and ask if you can identify the photograph.

A: Yes, Ma'am.

Q: What is that a photograph of?

A: Of a house Sherman was living in Dallas.

Q: That's where he lived in '97?

A: Yes, Ma'am.

Q: That's where you went in Dallas?

A: Yes, Ma'am.

MS. GRIFFIN: We move to admit Government's Exhibit Number 13.

Q: Why did you go to his house in Dallas?

A: At the point in time, I was visiting, at first. I was visiting him, you know, and also to pick up a package later on during the week.

Q: While you were visiting Sherman Williams at his house in Texas, what did you do connected with drugs?

A: Well . . .

Q: I can hardly hear you.

A: Well, about day later, you know, I guess he made his contact, and we went and picked up some marijuana.

Q: Who went and picked it up?

A: Sherman and I.

Q: Who paid for the marijuana?

A: Sherman did.

Q: About how much was it?

A: About eight thousand dollars.

Q: Eight thousand dollars?

A: Yes, Ma'am.

Q: How many pounds was that?

A: Twenty pounds.

Q: What did you do with that marijuana?

A: Put it in the trunk of the car and, later on that night, I proceeded home.

Q: Home being Mobile?

A: Yes, Ma'am.

Q: Then what happened to the marijuana?

A: I waited until he got there—he left some with me, and he took some somewhere else.

Q: Waited until who got to Mobile?

A: Waited until Sherman got to Mobile.

Q: How much of the marijuana did you give to Sherman?

A: Between fifteen . . . well, I would say between ten and fifteen pounds of it.

Q: What did you do with the remainder of the marijuana?

A: I tried to sell some of it myself. That's the way I had to get paid.

Q: Did you sell some of the marijuana?

A: Yes, I did.

Q: Did you pay Sherman Williams for some of it that you sold?

A: Yes, Ma'am.

Q: How much money did you pay him?

A: Well, in all—what I had to give him—was about . . . I would say about six or seven thousand dollars.

Q: What were you selling the pounds of marijuana for in '97?

A: Eight hundred dollars.

Q: Eight hundred dollars a pound?

A: Yes, Ma'am.

Q: Now, Mr. Freeman, did there come a time when you made a second trip to transport marijuana for Sherman Williams?

A: Yes, Ma'am.

Q: When was that?

A: I would say about two weeks later in '97.

Q: Still in '97?

A: Yes, Ma'am.

Q: Why did you make that trip? Who asked you to make that trip?

A: Him and I talked about . . . Sherman and I talked about, you know, I had lost my job, so I wasn't doing nothing.

Q: Where did you go the second time?

A: I went back up to his house at first—his mom was there, so he wanted me to go stay at a hotel.

Q: Now, when you said his house, whose house are you talking about?

A: Sherman's house.

Q: Did you stay at a hotel?

A: Yes, Ma'am.

Q: Did you receive any marijuana on that second trip?

A: After, we left to go to a football game. They had a preseason game that day.

Q: Did you ultimately receive some marijuana on that trip?

A: Yes, Ma'am.

Q: How much?

A: Another twenty pounds.

Q: Twenty pounds?

A: Yes, Ma'am.

Q: Who gave you the money for the marijuana?

A: Sherman did.

Q: What did you do with that marijuana?

A: Drove it back to Mobile.

Q: Did anyone come with you?

A: No Ma'am.

Q: What happened with the twenty pounds of marijuana once you got to Mobile?

A: He made some contacts—some calls—and some people picked up some, and I kept some.

Q: Okay. Who made some contacts and some calls?

A: Sherman did.

Q: What happened with the twenty pounds?

A: Waited to be distributed and sold.

Q: Pardon?

A: We . . . you know, he distributed some, and I sold

some.

Q: Again, what did you sell it for per pound?

A: I was selling it from eight hundred to nine hundred dollars a pound. That's the way I had to make money.

Q: Did you give any of those proceeds from the few pounds you kept to Sherman Williams?

A: Yes, Ma'am.

Q: Now, Mr. Freeman, did you make a third trip?

A: Yes, I did.

Q: Approximately when was that in '99?

A: It was like around . . . it was between July and August, somewhere up in there.

Q: Did anyone go with you?

A: No, Ma'am.

Q: How did you get there?

A: I drove a rental car.

Q: Who gave you the money for the rental car?

A: Sherman gave me the money for the rental car, at first, you know, and I also kept some money myself. He was supposed to have reimbursed me for paying for the rental car myself.

Q: You make reference to that in the video at your house about the rental car, is that right?

A: Yes, Ma'am.

Q: On this trip when you had the rental car, how much marijuana did you get in Texas?

A: Another twenty pounds.

Q: Pardon me?

A: Another twenty pounds.

Q: Had you tried to get more than twenty pounds?

A: Yes, Ma'am.

Q: What happened?

A: Didn't go through.

Q: Why was that?

A: Didn't have them. The man—I guess the man didn't have it.

Q: Who gave you the money for this twenty pounds before the last fifty pounds?

A: Sherman.

Q: Did you get twenty pounds?

A: Yes. Ma'am, I got twenty pounds.

Q: What did you do with it?

A: I drove it back to Mobile.

Q: What did you do with it once you got to Mobile?

A: Same old routine—kept some, and distributed some.

Q: Who did you give the marijuana to?

A: Sherman, when he came in.

Q: So, Mr. Freeman, Sherman never transported the marijuana himself from Texas to Mobile, is that correct?

A: No, Ma'am.

Q: Why was that?

A: That's just the way he was doing things, you know? I don't know . . .

Q: Did you consider that was your marijuana, or it was Sherman Williams's?

A: If it was mine, I would be getting all the proceeds from it, period. It wasn't mine.

Q: Mr. Freeman, when Sherman Williams was in your house on April the 21st, did he ask you about police coming back?

A: Yes, Ma'am.

Q: In other words, did he ask you if you saw police on the trip from Texas to Mobile?

A: Yes, Ma'am.

Q: What did you tell him?

A: I told him no, I didn't.

Q: In connection with his being in your house, did he ask you about . . . did he tell you he still got the old boy's money?

A: Yes, Ma'am.

Q: Who did you understand him to be talking about?

A: I knew he was talking about Rice.

Q: Why was that?

A: He didn't get his package, so he kept the money.

Q: And, you say, "For real, sorry he couldn't get his yoda." What were you talking about?

A: Cocaine.

Q: What is 'yoda' a street slang for?

A: Cocaine.

Q: During the course of his being at your house, you called him Shake?

A: Yes.

Q: Is that his nickname?

A: Yes, Ma'am.

Q: And, during the course of his being at your house, you saw him using a telephone. Was that your phone?

A: Yes, Ma'am.

Q: Does he appear to go from the top to the bottom, the top to the bottom at the end of the numbers?

A: Yes, Ma'am.

Q: Do you know if the 2-0 fits, or Shake 20?

A: Yes, Ma'am.

Q: Did you see him doing that when he would go top to bottom, top to bottom, back and forth?

A: Yes, Ma'am. I know the code. We both have codes.

Q: What's the purpose of having a code?

A: To know exactly who is calling.

Q: In other words, you might not be at your home when you were paging Sherman Williams, but you had a code to let him know it was you.

A: Yes, Ma'am.

Q: What was your code?

A: Forty-seven.

Q: What was Sherman Williams's code?

A: Twenty.

Q: You also make reference to Dee in the video. Who was Dee?

A: One of his girlfriends.

Q: That's the female whose picture you identified in the picture with you and Sherman Williams.

A: Yes, Ma'am.

Q: You also said if you left it in the car, it would be stinking. What were you talking about?

A: The garbage bag full of marijuana.

Q: Mr. Freeman, did you keep any of the fifty pounds of marijuana, or did Sherman Williams leave with all of it?

A: He left with all of it I would say, except for like a little quarter bag.

Q: Just before Mr. Williams left, did he give you a story to tell about taking clothes to your mother's house?

A: Yes, Ma'am.

Q: Were there some children outside?

A: Yes, Ma'am.

Q: Who came up with that story to say?

A: He did.

Q: When you said, "Oh, do you want me to still take those clothes to your mama's house," what were you doing?

A: I was just standing up outside.

Q: Where were the bags of marijuana?

A: Still in the house.

Q: How many bags of marijuana?

A: Forty-seven.

Q: Did Sherman leave with the bags?

A: Yes, Ma'am.

Q: Mr. Freeman, did the officers come in and take the small amount of marijuana that was left in the apartment?

A: Yes, Ma'am.

Q: And, was Mr. Williams ultimately arrested?

A: Yes, Ma'am.

Q: So, did Mr. Williams leave the black bag that you previously identified in your residence?

A: Yes, Ma'am.

Q: What was in the black bag?

A: Some clothes, and some money.

Q: Was there also a telephone?

A: Yes, Ma'am.

Q: What did you do with the contents of that black bag?

A: Well, I left the clothes and his phone in the bag.

Q: What did you do with the money?

A: I got the money out of there.

Q: How much money was it?

A: Alright. Before I didn't get a chance to finish counting it, but it was like about twenty something.

Q: Did you take some money from that bag?

A: Yes, Ma'am.

Q: Was that the money Kenneth Rice gave Sherman Williams? The money Sherman Williams brought into your home?

A: Yes, Ma'am.

Q: And, you admitted to the officers that you took some money from that bag, is that correct?

A: Yes, Ma'am. I was wrong, though.

Q: Those were drug proceeds? Excuse me, money to be used to buy cocaine?

A: Yes, Ma'am.

Q: You were not entitled to that money, were you?

A: No, Ma'am.

Q: And, you have plead guilty to taking that government

property?

A: Yes, I did.

Q: Now, you have also entered into an agreement to pay restitution to the United States.

A: Yes, Ma'am.

Q: For the money you took?

A: Yes, Ma'am.

MS. GRIFFIN: One moment—Your Honor, I show you Government's Exhibit 14.

Q: Mr. Freeman, I ask if you can identify the individual in Government's Exhibit 14.

A: Yes, Ma'am.

Q: Who is that a photograph of?

A: Demetrius Sanders.

Q: How did you know Demetrius Sanders?

A: I met him through Sherman.

Q: Okay—how is it you met Demetrius Sanders through Sherman? What circumstances?

A: We were going—we went to Dallas to pick up some marijuana.

Q: He went with you on one of the trips?

A: Yes, Ma'am.

Q: At whose direction did he go?

A: Huh?

Q: At whose direction did he go?

A: I-10 . . .

Q: I can't hear you.

A: Down 98 to 1-10.

Q: Who sent Mr. . . .

MS. GRIFFIN: Your Honor, we move to admit Government's Exhibit 14.

Q: Which trip did he go on to Dallas with you?

A: The fourth trip.

Q: You were then stopped on your last trip. He didn't go on that one?

A: No Ma'am.

Q: Did he go on the one just before then?

A: Yes, Ma'am.

Q: And, I'll show you Government's Exhibit 15, and ask if you can identify the exhibit.

A: Demetrius Thomas.

Q: That's a photograph of Demetrius Thomas?

A: Yes, Ma'am.

Q: How did you know Demetrius Thomas?

A: Through Sherman.

Q: How did you meet him through Sherman?

A: He came to my house.

Q: Who came to your house?

A: Sherman and Demetrius, and Demetrius.

Q: Demetrius Sanders and Demetrius Thomas?

A: Yes, Ma'am.

MS. GRIFFIN: We move to admit Government's Exhibit 15.

Q: Why was Demetrius Thomas coming to your house with Demetrius Sanders and Sherman Williams?

A: Because all four of us were suppose to be going to Dallas to pick up some more marijuana.

Q: I'm sorry, tell me one more time . . .

A: All of us were suppose to have been going to Dallas to pick up some more marijuana.

Q: Now, did you make a trip with Demetrius Sanders, Demetrius Thomas, and yourself to pick up marijuana in Texas?

A: Yes, Ma'am.

Q: What happened on that trip?

A: That trip, Sherman and I stayed at Dee's house. And, Shack and both of the Demetriuses—and, Dee—went to pick up some marijuana.

Q: Demetrius Sanders, or Demetrius Thomas?

A: Both. And, they was with the young lady, Dee.

Q: Now, you used the word, 'Shack.' Who do you know as Shack?

A: Demetrius Thomas.

Q: Did Demetrius Sanders have a nickname?

A: Meechie.

Q: Has Demetrius Sanders since drowned?

A: Yes, Ma'am.

Q: He is not living, is he?

A: No, Ma'am.

MS. GRIFFIN: That's all I have from this witness at this time.

THE COURT: Alright. Cross examination, Mr. Clark.

MR. CLARK: Yes, Sir, Judge.

MS. GRIFFIN: Judge, I omitted to ask a question.

THE COURT: Go ahead.

MS GRIFFIN:

Q: On the trip with Demetrius Sanders and Demetrius Thomas, did you see Sherman Williams in Texas?

A: Yes, Ma'am. We rode over together.

Q: To get out there?

A: Yes, Ma'am.

Q: What were you going to get on that trip?

A: Some marijuana.

Q: And, what happened on that trip?

A: Both of the Demetriuses and the young lady got robbed.

Q: What young lady?

A: Demetric. Dee.

Q: Demetrius Sanders and Demetrius Thomas got robbed, is that right?

A: Yes, Ma'am.

Q: So, where were you and Sherman Williams when Demetrius Sanders, Demetrius Thomas, and Dee got robbed?

A: We was at Dee's house.

Q: How did you and Sherman Williams learn Demetrius Sanders, Demetrius Thomas, and Dee were robbed?

A: Well, I told him I felt like something was wrong, you know? Because I was just sitting there and I got very nauseous, and I told him. I said, "Sherman, man, something's wrong—something ain't right. About five minutes later, they called and told him they got robbed. All hell broke loose from there.

Q: So, do you know how much marijuana Demetrius Sanders, Demetrius Thomas, and Dee got for Sherman Williams?

A: I would say, like, about a hundred pounds.

Q: A hundred pounds?

A: Yes, Ma'am.

Q: And, was the money gone?

A: Yes, Ma'am.

Q: When Demetrius Thomas, Demetrius Sanders, and Dee came back to the apartment, was Sherman Williams mad at them?

A: Yes, Ma'am.

MS. GRIFFIN: That's all we have, Your Honor.

CROSS EXAMINATION

MR. CLARK:

Q: Mr. Freeman, my name is Bob Clark. I don't believe we have ever met before, have we?

A: No, Sir.

Q: Now, first of all, let's look at your plea agreement, if we could, please, Sir. Let me give you a copy because I'm going to ask you some questions about it.

THE COURT: Do you have an exhibit number, Mr. Clark?

MR. CLARK: Defendant's Exhibit 1. I will mark it.

Q: Now—you were arrested in Texas back in April of this year, is that correct?

A: Yes, Sir.

Q: Then you came back to Mobile. We have seen the video tape you made for the government, is that correct?

A: Yes, Sir.

Q: Now, at the time you made the video tape for the government, did you have an agreement with the government not to prosecute you?

A: No, Sir.

Q: Did you, at any time prior to May of—from April 21st on to May, I believe it was—did you have any kind of agreement with the government not to prosecute you?

A: No.

Q: Alright. Now, you were not arrested on the 21st at your house, were you?

A: No, Sir.

Q: In fact, the black bag or the money that was left at your house, you didn't tell the agents who went there about that money, did you?

A: I didn't, no—no attention to the bag. When after he left the house, I didn't pay no attention to the bag.

Q: Did you count the money?

A: Yeah, after I got back.

Q: Did you call the agents and say, "Hey, look—there's a substantial amount of money here."

A: No, I didn't.

Q: Did you try to steal the money?

A: No, I didn't try to steal the money. I looked at it as a gift. All the time I had went and didn't get shit, so, hey, I kept it.

Q: So, you didn't bother to tell the government you had

taken ten thousand dollars?

A: No, I didn't.

Q: Alright. Did the government come out to you and say, "Hey, look—we know there's a black bag and it's missing. Do you know anything about the black bag?"

A: Yes, Sir.

Q: Did you tell them the money was on top of a hot water heater?

A: Yes.

Q: Did you also tell them that was all the money you received?

A: At that time, yeah.

Q: You lied to them, didn't you?

A: Yes, I did.

Q: And, they left?

A: Yes.

Q: They believed you?

A: Yes.

Q: But, it was a lie.

A: Yeah.

Q: Now, in the kind of business you have been in, do you have to lie a lot?

A: In the kind of business?

Q: Yes, Sir.

A: It depends.

Q: Okay. So you lied to the officers at that time. And, subsequently, were you confronted about the lie you told them about the ten thousand dollars?

A: Well, it's like when I told them about the ten thousand dollars, you know? I didn't care at that point in time because the fact is, I lost everything else anyway.

Q: But, up to that point, up until they came back and confronted you about taking the ten thousand dollars, you had not been arrested, had you?

A: No, Sir.

Q: But, once they found out you stole ten thousand dollars and lied to them, they arrested you, didn't they?

A: No, Sir.

Q: In fact, you have plead guilty to that theft, haven't you?

A: Yes. I have.

Q: And, it was after you stole the money that you got indicted—or, you agreed to plead guilty, didn't you?

A: I plead guilty to everything I done right off the bat.

Q: Well, you weren't arrested right off the bat, were you?

A: From Texas to Mobile, I was in Texas custody.

Q: Well—but you didn't get arrested by the federal government when you got here, did you?

A: No, Sir, I didn't.

Q: Then you made that movie on the 21st—you didn't

get arrested, did you?

A: I guess not.

Q: They didn't arrest you toward the end of the month— you had not been arrested, had you?

A: No, Sir.

Q: It wasn't until they found out you stole their money that they arrested you, was it?

A: I have not been arrested.

Q: You didn't plead guilty to stealing federal money?

A: I plead guilty, but I have not gone to jail.

Q: Did they take you into custody, bring you down here, and book and fingerprint you? Did that happen?

A: Yes.

Q: That happened after they found out about the money you stole?

A: Well, it was bound to happen anyway because I already plead guilty.

Q: You hadn't plead guilty when they found out about the money, had you?

A: They found out about the money on Monday. That means right after the weekend passed, they found out about the money then.

Q: They found out you took some of their money, and then they came out and arrested you, didn't they? They took you down to jail . . .

A: No.

Q: What did they do with you when they went back to your house, and confronted you about stealing the money?

A: The same thing you're doing . . . questioning me.

Q: Okay. Were you subsequently indicted? After that, did you get indicted for it?

A: Yes, because I plead guilty for taking the money.

Q: Okay. You were arrested, you were brought down here, and you went before a magistrate—an initial appearance, did you not?

A: Yes, I did.

Q: And, you told that magistrate you would abide by the laws of the United States, the law of the State of Alabama, Mobile County, and all the laws—if he would let you get free on bond, didn't you?

A: No. They freed me on bond on their own recognizance.

Q: I understand. But, do you recall the condition of your bond being that you could not violate laws?

A: Yeah, I know that.

Q: Did you know the condition was you not violate federal or state law, county laws, or city laws?

A: I know all of that, too.

Q: That was a condition of your release, wasn't it?

A: Sure was.

Q: You told the judge, under oath, you would abide by those conditions, didn't you?

A: Yes, I did.

Q: But, you didn't, did you?

A: No, I didn't.

Q: Well, did you violate any laws after you swore that you wouldn't?

A: I violated. Yes, I did.

Q: Okay. Did you possess cocaine after you swore to the judge you wouldn't violate any laws?

A: In my system. Yes, Sir, I did.

Q: In your system?

A: Yes, I did.

Q: Had you taken cocaine and put it in your nose, or something?

A: Yes.

Q: When you held that cocaine?

A: I snorted it.

Q: You snorted it. So, prior to your snorting it, you were standing there holding it, weren't you?

A: No, I wasn't.

Q: It was on a mirror, or it was on something, wasn't it?

A: It was in a bag, and I grabbed it.

Q: It was in a bag, and you grabbed it?

A: Yeah. After you have seen all the things I've seen, you know, all the pressures I had to go through, then you'll understand it. Until then you don't.

Q: Okay. Well, I will just try to understand. Okay?

A: Yeah.

Q: But, you know you were doing wrong . . .

MS. GRIFFIN: We object to that.

THE COURT: Yeah. Go ahead. Don't get into details. Just focus.

MR. CLARK: I'm sorry, Judge, I can't hear, anymore.

THE COURT: I'm sorry. I'm too far from the mic. Just focus on whether or not he violated . . .

MR. CLARK: Yes, Sir.

THE COURT: Not all the details.

MR. CLARK: Yes, Sir. I understand.

Q: Okay. Now—you had a hearing before this judge here, did you not?

A: Yes, I did.

Q: And, you admitted you used cocaine, didn't you?

A: Yes, Sir, I did.

Q: At that time, did the judge put you under oath and ask you to swear to tell the truth?

A: Yes, he did.

Q: After that, did you use cocaine again?

A: After I got dirty the first time? No, I didn't.

Q: Okay. So on the first time you—September 5th was the first time you provided a dirty urine, wasn't it?

A: No. They said the first I provided dirty urine, I was still dirty with marijuana, knowing I hadn't smoked any marijuana. The second time I was suppose to have been dirty was from cocaine. They said that was a false positive from marijuana.

Q: Yes, Sir. Let me show you what's been filed in your case, and ask if you are familiar with the government making these allegations that you tested positive on September the 5th for cocaine.

A: Yeah.

Q: Did you test positive for cocaine?

A: Yes, Sir.

Q: Did you tell Judge Butler, the judge here today, you used cocaine?

A: Yes, Sir, I did.

Q: You admitted that to the court?

A: Yes, Sir, I did.

Q: Now, on November the 14th, there was another blood test, wasn't there? Or, a urine test?

A: Yeah. I give UAs all the time.

Q: On that test, did you test positive for cocaine?

A: I don't know. Did I suppose to? Because if I did, they suppose to have arrested me.

Q: Have you been brought before—did you tell your probation officer or pretrial services officer you did cocaine?

A: My pretrial services officer.

Q: Did you tell your pretrial services officer that you—after he confronted you with the dirty urine, did you tell him you had used cocaine?

A: I told him I used cocaine before. Because my pretrial officer now is in Minneapolis . . .

Q: Okay. Now, then, back on November 14th, were you in Minneapolis?

A: Yeah. I was in Minneapolis.

Q: Did you test dirty for cocaine?

A: He did not bring it to my attention about me testing for no cocaine.

Q: And, you didn't admit to the pretrial officer you used cocaine, is that right? Is that what you're telling us?

A: I'm telling you he did not bring it to my attention.

Q: Well, did you discuss it with him—the dirty urine—on November 14th?

A: I discussed it with him—my pressure, and my mind. What was going on in my life, my family, and what I'm missing.

Q: Yes, Sir. But on the 14th, did you take a urine test?

A: I'm telling you what I did.

Q: Okay. Did you take a urine test on the 14th?

A: I don't know what day I probably took it on because it's like I called in my color. Whatever my color is, that's when I go.

Q: Did your probation officer call you, or your pretrial services officer call you in to discuss your test with you?

A: No, he didn't. I told him I was coming home for Thanksgiving. I told him I was—I had to come back here on December 4th.

Q: What did you have to come back here on December 4th for?

A: Court.

Q: Because of the second urine test, wasn't it?

A: Today is December the 4th.

Q: Yes, Sir. But, it's been out of here, hasn't it?

A: No. What I was suppose to have came to court for is because I got my subpoena in the mail saying this here's court day.

Q: Alright. You have another court date, do you not, Sir, wherein—

A: I don't know when is my court date, Sir.

Q: I understand. But, you do have a court date for a second dirty urine, don't you?

A: Sir, I don't know that. Nothing about that. I'm trying to tell you that now.

Q: Yes, Sir.

A: You keep asking me the same question.

THE COURT: Yeah. Mr. Clark, let me say, you need to either . . .

MR. CLARK: Move on. I will move on, Judge.

THE COURT: Well, you can stay on the subject, but just get on a new area of the same subject.

MR. CLARK:

Q: Do you know why Ms. Dow—sitting here at the end of the table—would file a motion to revoke your claiming you had dirty urine on November 14th? Do you know why she would do that if it's not true?

A: Well, she hadn't brought nothing like that to my attention. I met with her when I first got here, and she hasn't said anything to me about it. You know what I'm saying?

MR. CLARK: Judge, we would like to have this marked as . . .

THE COURT: So, counsel.

MR. CLARK: Yes, Sir.

MS. GRIFFIN: May we approach?

THE COURT: Well, mark it first, and then we'll see what it is. Mark it in.

MR. CLARK:

Q: Mr. Freeman, let's talk about your plea agreement, if we could please, Sir. You were represented by an attorney, Mr. Christopher Knight, at the time you signed your plea agreement, were you not ?

A: Yes.

Q: Pardon?

A: Yes.

Q: And, you entered this plea agreement back in . . . July 26th of 2000. It's in front of you. If you need to refresh your recollection in any way, look at it, okay?

A: I know what I plead.

Q: Yes, Sir. I just mean if you need to look at it, feel free to do so. Mr. Christopher Knight represented you at the plea, did he not ?

A: Yes, he did.

Q: He went over this with you, and told you that the range of punishment was five to four years, did he not?

A: Yes.

Q: Okay. Did you discuss with him what you would get out of this if you entered a plea, and agreed to testify?

A: Yes.

Q: What did you discuss with him?

A: Said they might look at it on the lower guidelines.

Q: What does that mean? Mr. Freeman, you went to a probation conference, did you not?

A: Yeah.

Q: Where they explained the guidelines to you?

A: Yeah.

Q: Okay. What were your guidelines?

A: Like, twenty-something, thirty-something.

Q: Okay. Did they tell you they would cut that in half if you would agreed to testify?

A: They said they would try to drop it down as low as possible.

Q: Did the term 'one-half' rear it's ugly head any time during that conversation with your lawyer?

A: Yeah. I had that conversation with my lawyer.

Q: Okay. So—he told you if you agreed to testify, you would get one-half the time you had to serve off, is that right?

A: Maybe. That still depends on the judge.

Q: Maybe, but that was your understanding, wasn't it?

A: Don't make any difference. I know I'm guilty. I'm going to have to do something.

Q: Okay. Now, in your plea agreement, on page three it says you will provide substantial assistance, doesn't it?

A: Yes.

Q: And, you discussed that with your lawyer, didn't you?

A: Yes.

Q: He said simply telling on people, you know, is not good enough—you have to get somebody convicted, didn't he?

A: It don't make no difference if I help get anybody get convicted or not. And, you know that as well as the court know that, as well as he knows. He's guilty as well as I was. I can't afford it. Where am I going to get it from? I don't know nobody in Texas.

Q: Anything else?

A: I'm not from Texas.

Q: Anything else you want to say?

A: Yes—I'm from Alabama. All of these questions you're asking me still ain't going to make a world of difference.

Q: Okay.

A: Because the government know as well as I know, he's guilty, I'm guilty. Everybody that's involved is guilty.

Q: Yes, Sir. But, my question to you, Sir—when you made this agreement to testify, you knew the more people you got convicted, the better it was going to be for you, didn't you?

A: It's not about more people—it's just who I was testifying against, Sherman Williams. I don't know nothing about nobody else.

Q: Well, they didn't just say that you provided assistance. You had to provide substantial assistance, didn't you?

A: Substantial assistance.

Q: Alright. Now, you admit you lied to the people when they came out and talked to you about the money, didn't you?

A: Yes.

Q: And, you lied to the judge when you promised not to use drugs, didn't you?

A: Yes.

Q: So, you've made several lies to court officials, to this judge here, other judges, DEA—you lied to those people, haven't you?

A: Yes, I have. And, I have also corrected my lies to the right.

Q: Okay. Now, in your plea agreement on panel four, it says you will agree to take a polygraph test, doesn't it?

A: Yeah.

Q: Has a polygraph test been given to you?

A: No, it hasn't.

Q: So the government never has come and said, "Look, we think you're lying because you've lied so many times—we want to give you a polygraph," did they? Did they?

A: Well, they wanted to give me a polygraph, and I told them there's no need for that. I don't have to lie. For what?

Q: But you admit you have lied. You lied to this court and . . .

THE COURT: Don't go over that.

MR. CLARK. Okay. I'm sorry, Judge.

Q: Okay. Alright. Now, you say you didn't know anybody in Texas. Is that what you told us?

A: Correct.

Q: Alright. Now, did you know Roderick Ward?

A: Yes.

Q: You've known Roderick Ward since grammar school, haven't you?

A: I would say, like, about since high school.

Q: Since high school. Mr. Ward dropped out of high school, didn't he?

A: Yes.

Q: And, Mr. Ward was arrested for dealing drugs, wasn't he?

A: I guess so, yeah.

Q: Well, you knew he got arrested. He went to the penitentiary, didn't he?

A: His life wasn't involved with my life. I was a football player. He wasn't a football player. He wasn't nothing. He's a nobody. I don't know . . .

Q: But, you knew him.

A: Of him.

Q: And, you knew he got in trouble.

A: Everybody did.

Q: Alright. Then, in 1997, Mr. Williams was playing for the Dallas Cowboys, wasn't he?

A: True.

Q: And, you went out there to see—in the year 1997, how many times did you go out there to see the game?

A: One preseason game.

Q: Okay.

A: That wasn't in 1997. That was in 1998.

Q: Well, did you go out there in 1997, or am I mistaken?

A: Between . . . yeah. At the end of '97, and the beginning of '98, right before his birthday.

Q: Well, did you tell Ms. Griffin on direct the first time you went to Dallas, Texas was in 1997? Let's see . . .

A: Visiting.

Q: Pardon? Him?

A: Yes, Sir. I stayed at his house.

Q: You stayed at Sherman Williams's house?

A: Yes, Sir.

Q: With his girlfriend? The '97 trip?

A: With her cousins.

Q: Pardon?

A: I stayed at his house with his girlfriend and her cousins.

Q: And, you told us you traveled to Texas by yourself.

A: Yes, I did.

Q: You went to his house in Dallas.

A: Yeah. He wired me some money through the Western Union to get a rental car.

Q: Okay. And, you went—so, in 1997, you went to his house in Dallas.

A: It's the same question again.

Q: Okay. Do you recall what month that was that you went to Dallas?

A: It was like around June or July—somewhere up there. No later than August.

Q: Alright. And . . .

A: It was in June and July because he was in camp.

Q: He was practicing, is that correct?

A: Right.

Q: And, that was the season Emmitt Smith wasn't signed, and they were really looking at Sherman.

MS. GRIFFIN: Objection, Your Honor, as to relevance.

THE COURT: Overruled.

MR. CLARK:

Q: They were looking at Sherman Williams to replace Emmitt Smith, weren't they?

A: Not really. I don't know. Well, Sherman could never replace Emmitt Smith. Not in my recollection.

Q: Well, Emmitt Smith missed some of the games of the 1997 season, didn't he?

A: Injury. Yeah.

Q: Sherman Williams filled in for him, didn't he?

A: His job.

Q: And, Sherman Williams was making good money at that time, wasn't he?

A: I don't want his money.

Q: I didn't ask you if you wanted his money, Sir.

A: What does money got to do with—

THE COURT: Was he making money? Do you know?

THE WITNESS: He was making money. Everybody knew how much money he was making. When he signed the contract, it was publicized on TV.

MR. CLARK:

Q: Alright. And, you went out to see him because you knew he had money, and you didn't.

A: Look here—money don't make my world.

MR CLARK: Judge, I ask the witness to answer the question.

THE COURT: No. No. Just answer his question, if you answer it yes or no. Go ahead, restate your question . . .

THE WITNESS: Yeah, he got money. I'm proud of him.

MR. CLARK:

Q: And, you went out to see him knowing he was a Dallas Cowboy, and he had money, didn't you?

THE COURT: Is that why you went to see him, or did you go for some other reason?

THE WITNESS: No, I went for another reason.

MR. CLARK:

Q: Okay.

A: A better reason. Friend, I thought, anyway. We wouldn't even be in this crap if he wouldn't have lied.

THE COURT: I think he answered the question. Go ahead, Mr. Clark.

MR. CLARK:

Q: Well, what did you say about a lie?

A: We wouldn't even be in this crap if he wasn't a lie. Before we left Mobile, I asked Sherman Williams where is Shack, where is Demetrius Thomas. Guess what he told me? The man is at home. So, I guess his home was in jail. You rarely see a man when you already know another man is in jail—because I wouldn't have even let him went. I would have tried to talk him out of it. Now, ask him that.

MR. CLARK: Was that the answer to some question I asked, Judge?

THE COURT: Go ahead with your next question, Mr. Clark.

MR. CLARK:

Q: Now, in 1997, when you went to Texas, did you meet a lady by the name of Demetric Beans?

A: Yeah, we did.

Q: Did you ever see her without Sherman present?

A: After he left that morning.

Q: Did she have a pet name for you? Pervert?

A: Yeah.

Q: Tell the ladies and gentlemen of the jury where she came up with the name, Pervert?

A: Our sexual intercourse.

THE COURT: Now, Mr. Clark, I'm going to interpose at this point. I don't think you need to go any further in that area.

MR. CLARK: Okay.

Q: So, you were—could we say you were close with Ms. Beans?

A: You don't have to get close with nobody to get you a groove.

Q: No, Sir. I'm saying that . . .

A: You don't have to be close to anybody to get your groove on.

Q: You became friends with Ms. Beans?

A: Acquaintance.

Q: Okay. You became an acquaintance with Ms. Beans, and this was in the summer of 1997?

A: I guess so. No, well . . . that was after my second visit up there. In 1997, yeah.

Q: Okay, I thought you told us earlier you only went out there one time in 1997. Are you saying it's twice?

A: I did not tell you that.

Q: Okay. I said I thought you said that. Are you telling us now you went out there twice?

A: You're suppose to know this, Sir.

THE COURT: Just answer the question. Don't argue with him.

THE WITNESS: He keeps asking me the same questions.

THE COURT: Mr. Freeman, don't argue with him. Just answer the question as best you can. He said, "Did you go out there more than once in 1997?"

THE WITNESS: Yes, I did.

THE COURT: Okay.

MR. CLARK:

Q: Well, tell us, when Ms. Griffin was asking you questions you said the first trip. You said the first trip, 1997, was the first trip you went to Texas by yourself. You went to his home in Dallas. Then, she asked you the next time you went. The second trip, that was the time you stayed at the hotel. Did you tell us that was in '97 or 1998?

A: In '97. I stayed there at the motel. That's when I met Dee.

Q: Okay. And, what month was that?

A: It was, like, about two or three weeks after, while he was still in training.

Q: Okay. And, his mother was out there at that time, was she not?

A: Yes, she was.

Q: He was staying at his house with his mother?

A: And, his girlfriend. Because I pulled up outside, he came, got in the car with me, and he carried me to the Days Inn Hotel.

Q: Okay. Where did you meet Ms. Beans?

A: Through him, probably.

Q: No—where did you meet her?

A: Honestly, at this point in time, I don't remember exactly where I met her at.

Q: Did you meet her at her condo?

A: Probably did. I don't remember, exactly.

Q: Well, you knew she had a condo, didn't you?

A: Yeah.

Q: You have been to that condo, haven't you?

A: Well, she done moved from where she use to stay, from now. You know, where I first met her at, it's not the same apartment she's at now.

Q: So, you knew where she use to live, and you know where she lives now?

A: Yeah.

Q: Did you and Roderick ever go out to Dallas to see Ms. Beans?

A: Me and Roderick Ward ain't never went nowhere together.

Q: Okay. Did you and Mr. Ward work at Shake 20?

A: I don't know what kind of work Ward did at Shake 20, but, on occasions, I have opened the studio up, you know, for somebody to come in there—to have a little party there.

Q: Okay. Did you work for Shake 20?

A: Involved in Shake 20?

Q: Yes, Sir.

A: No. He didn't do that. He didn't do that for me. I was just his little flunky.

THE COURT: You've got a little more to go, I see.

MR. CLARK: Yes, Sir. Yes, Sir. l have a lot . . .

THE COURT: Okay. Well, let's recess, Ladies and Gentlemen. We've had a long day. I want to visit with you a minute. Mr. Freeman, you can step down, if you will, please, Sir. You will be back in the morning for further examination.

THE COURT: Ladies and Gentlemen, before you leave tonight let me tell you a couple of things. First of all, normally, in a lot of trials, the first witness is the longest witness. And, I know you're thinking, "Gosh, it's been half a day with this witness—how long are we going to be here?" Usually, not always, the witnesses tend to get shorter as we get on into the trial. But, I do want you to understand, you have not heard that witness's final testimony.

Like I told you—I think more than one today—it's real

important you keep an open mind about the case. And, sometimes that's hard to do. Thoughts creep into your head, and you begin to form opinions, and nobody can stop you from doing that. But, remember—there's going to be more evidence, there's going to be more testimony, there's going to be more cross-examination and, perhaps, redirect of this witness. So do your best to keep that human part of you in check, knowing you have to wait until all the evidence is in before you can make any decision in this case.

Now, when you go home tonight, your husband, wife, whomever you talk to, is going to want to know all about your day in court, and you're going to want to tell them everything. And, the minute you start telling them about it, they're probably going to give you their opinion—we know that happens. So, the best thing for you to do is tell them as little as you can—tell them what I am telling you now. Tell them you took an oath to try the case on the evidence and law you hear. That person whom you love so much is not going to be in the jury room with you and your fellow jurors.

So, when you leave this courthouse later in the week, the verdict you return needs to be your verdict. Whatever it is, you will have a clean conscience that you returned a verdict—no one else in your family. The more you stay away from that, the better you will feel about whatever verdict you reach.

I will also tell you there is a newspaper reporter and a television reporter in the courtroom for part of the day today, so there may be publicity about this case. Publicity is often governed by different rules than the rules of evidence. In fact, I will say it is different because media has a very short space in the newspaper column—or, time on a television story—to report what was seen or heard in the courtroom. Sometimes it emphasizes something one way or the other that might not have been important to you. So, it's best you avoid any contact with media exposure. I can tell you, there is going to be the news you want to see tonight on CNN about the Presidential election, and that might be a good channel to turn to.

Since we're at the end of the day, I will tell you the state judge in Tallahassee ruled in favor of Governor Bush that the recount, the manual recount should not go forward. Of course, that will be immediately appealed to the Florida Supreme Court. The U.S. Supreme Court sent the other decision back down, so there's going to be plenty for you to listen to on the other media and in the newspaper. When you pick up the paper in the morning and look at it, the minute you see anything about this case just fold it up—don't read it. So when you come back tomorrow, you will have the same open mind you've had throughout these proceedings. Every one of you has been attentive, alert, and conscientiously doing what we ask you to do—we appreciate it.

When you leave tonight, I'm going to ask you to fold up your notes—just put them on your chair. Ms. Kramer picks them up, and puts them in my office where they're locked up, Nobody looks at them. When you come back in the morning, they will be on your chair, and you can open them up, picking up right where you left off this morning.

I think we'll be able to start right at nine o'clock. I have other matters unrelated to this case starting at eight fifteen. Ms. Kramer and I will be here working on these other matters, and I think we'll finish up just before nine—then I'll call you up to start, so we need all fourteen of you to be here on time. If anybody is late, we have to hold up—so try to get here by a quarter to nine. That will allow you some extra time for traffic delays, or whatever.

Thank you for your hard work today—we'll see you in the jury assembly room downstairs. What you do now is check out in the jury clerk's office and, when you come back in the morning, you will check back in. Wait downstairs, and Mr. Smith will bring you back up.

Thank you, Ladies and Gentlemen.

We'll be in recess.

THOUGHTS

DECEMBER 5, 2000

After the trial's first day, I had plenty of time to reflect on the day's testimony as I lay on my bunk that night. I was somewhat heartened by family and friends attending the proceedings, and I was particularly happy to see my mother. No matter the situation, she stood at my side, never questioning the strength of our relationship. I recalled her cheering for me from the football stands, proud that her son achieved his dreams—and, that's what she wanted for me.

That's all she wanted.

Then, as guards signaled lights out for the night, I thought about Frank Freeman.

I admit it was tough hearing my friend mislead the judge and jury. When asked by the prosecuting attorney, he explained how and when we met—unfortunately, his statements were inaccurate and contradicting. I had no doubt his answers were influenced by the prosecution team, but, as I watched him on the witness stand, there was a dark pang in my heart as I realized our friendship had irreparably changed.

We were friends no more.

The following morning, my routine was the same as the previous day, but I had an opportunity to read a newspaper article recapping the first day of the trial. There was nothing opposing my recollection, but I had to smile when the reporter commented on how sharply I was dressed. Yes, it was a small thing, but the observation made me feel slightly better about things.

As I waited for the courtroom to come to order on the second day, concerns regarding how well my attorneys were presenting my case resurfaced. On the first day of the trial, I felt they should have objected to some of the contradictory statements made by government witnesses. Why they didn't, to this day I have no idea—all I knew was they didn't seem to have the same desire to win as the prosecuting team. It was a concern over which I had no control—no matter my conversations with my attorneys, they were set on their course.

Finally, it was time. Standing when the judge entered the courtroom, I glanced at the jury—maybe I could read their expressions. What they were thinking.

Nothing.

The Second Day

DECEMBER 5, 2000
UNITED STATES OF AMERICA (plaintiff) vs.
SHERMAN WILLIAMS (defendant)

THE COURT: Good morning, Mr. Clark. Proceed with your cross examination.

MR. CLARK: Yes, Sir, Judge.

FRANK FREEMAN

The witness, having been previously sworn to tell the truth, the whole truth and nothing but the truth, returned to the stand, was examined, and testified as follows:

CROSS EXAMINATION

MR. CLARK:

Q: Good morning, Mr. Freeman. I just have a couple of questions to ask you this morning. The first time you went to Dallas to see Sherman Williams was in 1997, was it not?

A: Yes, Sir.

Q: And, at that time, he was playing for the Dallas Cowboys.

A: Yes, Sir.

Q: He didn't come back to Mobile with you on any of these occasions, did he?

A: No, Sir.

Q: He was employed by the Cowboys, and he stayed in Dallas—most seasons, he stayed there until sometime in January, didn't he?

A: No, Sir, he didn't. He flew in. He would fly in, and then fly back there.

Q: I understand. His employment was in Dallas, Texas, wasn't it?

A: Yes, Sir.

Q: He practiced every day of the week but Tuesday, didn't he?

A: I don't know what days he practiced.

Q: Okay. Well, you say he flew back and forth to Mobile.

A: Yeah.

Q: During football season?

A: Yeah.

Q: How many days would you say he would stay at a time?

A: I don't know how long he stayed. He would stay around a couple of hours, and then he out.

Q: Okay. But, he had full-time employment with the Dallas Cowboys in '97, didn't he?

A: Yes, Sir.

Q: And, '98?

A: Yes, Sir.

Q: In '99 he went to work full time with the Mobile Admirals, didn't he?

A: For a little while, yeah.

Q: Then he went back to Dallas.

A: Yeah—I guess so.

Q: He had a full time job with the Dallas Cowboys, didn't he?

A: Well, from my recollection, he didn't play at all times on Dallas because he was on, like, a practice roster.

Q: Uh-huh.

A: Because I followed the game. I love the game.

Q: But, he had employment in the year 1999, didn't he?

A: Yeah.

Q: Okay. Now, in the year 2000, he asked you to help him move Tabitha Scott, his girlfriend, back to Mobile, didn't he?

A: No, he didn't.

Q: Did you ever go to Texas with Sherman to move Ms. Scott back?

A: No, I didn't.

Q: Do you know whether or not Ms. Scott ever moved back?

A: Yes, I do.

Q: Did she move back?

A: Yes, she did.

Q: Do you know how her furniture got back here?

A: No, I do not.

Q: You don't know it was hauled back in a U-haul?

A: No, I didn't.

Q: You didn't have anything to do with that?

A: Nothing.

Q: Mr. Williams never paid you any money for that?

A: Nothing.

Q: Was it your testimony yesterday you never got any marijuana from Ms. Demetric Beans other than for personal use?

A: That's the only thing I ever got from her.

Q: You never got as much as a pound from her?

A: No, Sir, I didn't.

Q: Okay. Yesterday, do you recall the video and the transcript? The video taken at your home?

A: Yes, Sir.

Q: You lived there for how many years?

A: About five or six years.

Q: Who lived there with you?

A: My wife.

Q: Alright. You and your wife lived there for five or six years, and you set up this video, did you not?

A: Yes, I did.

Q: There was a transcript the government issued, is that right?

A: Yes, Sir, they did.

Q: Tell us when you viewed that video, and read the transcript.

A: I started reading it within the next week of it.

Q: The next week? What do you mean?

A: After it happened.

Q: You read the transcript?

A: No. The video. I watched the video, and started writing down the things that were said back and forth.

Q: Yes, Sir. But, when did you read the transcript and watch the video both?

A: When they had it completed.

Q: When was that, Sir?

A: I don't know. It was during all of this. During these months that's been passed by now.

Q: Okay. So, you don't know when you read the transcript, and watched the video?

A: Not the exact date.

Q: Okay. Do you recall where you were?

A: Do I know where I was when I was doing it?

Q: Yes, Sir.

A: Yes, Sir, I do.

Q: Where were you?

A: At the FBI building.

MR. CLARK: The FBI building. Okay. Judge, the only thing I have left . . . I think I need to talk. We need to have a sidebar.

THE COURT: Do you mind Mr. Howard?

MR. CLARK: No, Sir. Judge.

(An off-the-record discussion was held at sidebar)

MR. CLARK: That's all, Judge. Thank you.

THE COURT: Alright. Redirect.

REDIRECT EXAMINATION

MS. GRIFFIN:

Q: Mr. Freeman, what is the practice roster? What is the practice roster you were talking about?

A: It was, like, he was practicing, trying to make the team again, you know?

Q: He was on that in the fall of '99, is that right?

A: Yes, Ma'am.

Q: Now, he was cut in the fall of '99—is that correct?

A: Yeah. Trying to make the team again. He started playing special teams.

Q: After the fall of '99, he no longer played football?

A: No, Ma'am.

Q: So, from the fall of '99 to his arrest, he didn't have a job?

A: No, Ma'am.

Q: He was unemployed.

A: Yes, Ma'am.

Q: You plead guilty to two felonies—is that correct?

A: Yes, Ma'am, I have.

Q: Are you awaiting sentencing?

A: Yes, Ma'am, I am.

Q: Do you understand you have a revocation hearing pending?

A: Yes, Ma'am.

Q: I want to talk to you about being arrested. You were stopped in Texas on the 20th of April?

A: Yes, Ma'am.

Q: Were you taken into custody?

A: Yes, I was.

Q: Were handcuffs put on you?

A: Yes, Ma'am.

Q: Were you put in a police car?

A: Yes, Ma'am.

Q: You were transported to the police station?

A: Yes, Ma'am.

Q: Did you come back to Alabama of your own free will, or were you in the car with police officers?

A: I was in the car with police officers.

Q: We showed you your plea agreement yesterday—Mr. Clark introduced it. Did you also do a factual résumé where you admitted the facts to the court?

A: Yes, Ma'am.

Q: Is that your signature on Government's Exhibit 2, the factual résumé?

A: Yes, Ma'am.

Q: Is that what you signed and have read?

A: Yes, I have.

MS. GRIFFIN: Your Honor, we move to admit his factual résumé, Government's Exhibit 2.

MR. CLARK: Judge, could we have just a second?

(Pause)

MR. CLARK: We have no objection, Your Honor.

THE COURT: Mark it in.

(Government's Exhibit Number 2 received and marked into evidence)

MS. GRIFFIN:

Q: Did you read this before you signed it?

A: Yes.

Q: Does it state you are transporting that marijuana from Dallas to Sherman Williams's?

A: Yes, it does.

Q: Tell us what you meant yesterday when you told us about Shack's being in jail, and your having no knowledge of it.

A: Yes, Ma'am. If I knew that man was in jail, I wouldn't have even went.

Q: What do you mean? Who is Shack?

A: Shack was just a normal driver who also would go up there and pick up for Sherman.

Q: What is Shack's real name?

A: Demetrius Thomas.

Q: Is that the person depicted in Government's Exhibit 15?

A: Yes, Ma'am, it is.

Q: You did not know Demetrius Thomas was in jail?

A: No, Ma'am, I didn't.

Q: Why was Demetrius Thomas in jail?

A: Transporting marijuana.

Q: And, was he in jail in Texas at the time you went to Texas?

A: Yes, Ma'am, he was.

Q: Did you ask Sherman Williams about that before you went to Texas to pick up the marijuana?

A: Before I left my house, I asked him about it. He told me Shack was at home.

Q: Because you had not been running for Sherman Williams in 2000, had you?

A: No, Ma'am.

Q: Who had?

A: Shack.

Q: So, he asked you to go.

A: Yes, Ma'am. He came and asked me to volunteer to come. I knew something was wrong then, but I really didn't pay no attention.

Q: What upset you about Shack's being in jail?

A: I wouldn't have went. I won't offer for him to even go. I looked at him as other people don't look at him. As a friend. I have been around him all of my life, since second grade. People can say what they want. I mean, who I am, a friend—that's all I've ever been to him. A friend. I don't want nothing he have because I have all of my life. I can still get what I work for. I got myself involved in that—I did that.

Q: That's what upset you about your friendship with Sherman Williams?

A: Yes, Ma'am.

Q: That he would send you knowing one of his runners had already been caught?

A: Yes, Ma'am.

MS. GRIFFIN: That's all we've got.

THE COURT: Mr. Freeman, that concludes your testimony. Before you leave, let me explain this—don't discuss your testimony, what you testified about, or what the questions were the lawyers asked you with any other witness until after the trial is over. Then, if you want to, you can.

You may step down. Thank you, Sir.

(Witness left the stand)

THE COURT: Ladies and Gentlemen—I tell every witness the same thing I just told this witness. It doesn't matter if it's a criminal case or a civil case. I do it for the reason I think you will agree with—when a witness leaves, there are other witnesses out in the witness room and, sometimes, witnesses who are about to testify are curious about what just went on. They may say, "What did they ask you," as well as what was said.

We want every new witness to be unaffected by the testimony of the prior witness. It's not that I suspect the witnesses are going to try to get together to make up their stories. Every witness in every trial I tell that to whether the government calls the witness, or the defendant.

MRS. DOW: Government calls State Trooper Chris Baggett.

CHRIS BAGGETT

The witness, after having first been duly sworn to tell, the truth, the whole truth, and nothing but the truth, was examined and testified as follows:

MRS. DOW:

Q: Tell us your name.

A: My name is Chris Baggett.

Q: How are you employed?

A: I'm employed with the Texas Department of Public Safety and Highway Patrol Service.

Q: How long have you been employed as a Texas highway patrol officer?

A: I was employed August of '98.

Q: Do you remember stopping a Volkswagon Jetta on April 20th of 2000?

A: Yes, Ma'am.

Q: I'm going to show you what has been entered evidence as Government's Exhibit 1. Can you identify it please?

A: Yes, Ma'am. That will be the Volkswagon we stopped on the 20th of April.

Q: Where was the stop made?

A: In Texas, on Interstate 20 east bound in Van Zandt County around the 530 mile marker.

Q: Is that close to Tyler, Texas?

A: Yes, Ma'am.

Q: Approximately what time was the stop made?

A: I believe the stop was around 4:55 P.M.

Q: In what direction was the Volkswagon going?

A: It was eastbound.

Q: Who was in the Jetta?

A: Frank Freeman and Mark Mixon.

Q: I'm going to show you what has been entered into evidence as Government's Exhibit 7. Can you identify those individuals?

A: Yes, Ma'am. The gentleman on the left would be Mr. Frank Freeman.

Q: That was the person driving the Jetta?

A: Yes, Ma'am.

Q: After stopping the Jetta, what did you do?

A: We had Mr. Freeman exit the vehicle, and spoke with him. When Mr. Freeman exited the vehicle, we smelled an overwhelming odor of green marijuana. So, we went ahead and spoke with Mr. Freeman, and asked for consent to search.

Q: Why did you stopped the Jetta?

A: Mr. Freeman, when he passed us, he drifted—I can't remember. It's in my report. He either drifted from the outside lane to the inside lane, or the outside lane to the inside lane. He drifted across the center stripe, and back.

Q: So, after observing this irregular driving pattern, you stopped him?

A: Yes, Ma'am.

Q: I'm going to show you what has been marked as Government's Exhibit 47. Can you identify Government's Exhibit 47 for us, please?

A: Yes, Ma'am. That's a video and audio tape of the stop we conducted on that day.

Q: The stop of Frank Freeman?

A: Yes, Ma'am.

Q: And, you have viewed Government's Exhibit 47?

A: Yes, Ma'am.

Q: Does Government's Exhibit 47 fairly and accurately depict the events of that traffic stop?

A: Yes, Ma'am.

MS. DOW: The government would move to enter into evidence Government's Exhibit 47.

MR. CLARK: No objection.

THE COURT: Mark it in.

MS. DOW: The government would ask to publish . . .

THE COURT: Go ahead.

MS. DOW: . . . a portion of Government's Exhibit 47.

(Government's Exhibit 47 was played in open court before the jury.)

MRS. DOW:

Q: I want to point out what has been marked as Government's Exhibit 11, a map of a portion of highway in Texas. Can you point out Tyler, Texas on the map?

THE COURT: Well, you point it out, Ms. Dow. It's obvious where it is. We don't need the . . . just point it out.

MRS. DOW:

Q: Is that the area he . . . Frank Freeman, was stopped in?

A: Actually, he was stopped a little bit west of there, about dead center.

Q: A little this way?

THE COURT: West, Ms. Dow.

MS. DOW:

Q: Right here?

A: Yes, Ma'am.

Q: After speaking to Frank Freeman, you said you asked to search the Jetta, is that correct ?

A: Yes, Ma'am.

Q: Did you search the Jetta?

A: Yes, Ma'am.

Q: Can you describe what you found in the search of the Jetta?

A: In the trunk, we found two trash bags, each of which contained approximately twenty-five pounds of marijuana. They were packaged individually in Ziplock baggies, fifty pounds total.

Q: What did you do after finding the marijuana in the trunk of the vehicle?

A: We placed Mr. Mixon and Mr. Freeman under arrest, Mirandized them, counted out the bundles of marijuana, placed them back in the plastic bags, and placed them in our patrol car.

Q: Now, I want to show you what has been marked as Government's Exhibit 24(a). Can you identify Government's Exhibit 24(a)?

A: Yes, Ma'am. That would be the marijuana that was located in the trunk of the Jetta.

Q: I am going to show you what has been marked as Government's Exhibit 24(b). Can you identify Government's

Exhibit 24(b)?

A: Yes, Ma'am. Those appear to be the trash bags it was contained in.

Q: Also in Government's Exhibit 24(b), what are the smaller bags?

A: Those would be the Ziplock baggies each bundle was in.

Q: So, 24(a) was contained in 24(b)?

A: Yes, Ma'am.

Q: You testified that you placed the—you took the bags out, and you examined the garbage bags and the contents. Then what did you do with them?

A: They were secured in our vehicle—in the patrol vehicle, in the trunk.

Q: And what did you do at that point with Mark Mixon and Frank Freeman?

A: They were both taken to the DPS office in Canton.

Q: What did you do with the Volkswagon?

A: The Volkswagon Jetta was inventoried and towed by Tommy's Wrecker Service.

Q: When you got to the area—where did you take them to be interviewed?

A: To the DPS office there in Canton.

Q: And, when you arrived at the office, where was the marijuana?

A: We took it from the trunk and placed it in our office

Q: And, was it secured?

A: Yes, Ma'am.

Q: Did there come a time when it was placed back in the trunk of the Jetta?

A: Yes, Ma'am. Whenever Sergeant Dunklin decided they were going to take everything—the case was going to be brought over here to Alabama, and he was going to meet with Alabama State Police. Trooper Rorman, my partner, and I had Tommy's Wrecker Service bring the Jetta back to our office. We then placed the marijuana in the back of the Jetta as it was when we found it.

Q: And, are Government's Exhibits 24(a) and (b) in substantially the same condition today as they came into your custody on April the 20th?

A: Yes, Ma'am.

Q: Who interviewed Frank Freeman?

A: Sergeant Dunklin.

MS. DOW: The Government has no further questions for this witness.

THE COURT: Alright. Mr. Clark?

MR. CLARK: Just a few, Judge.

CROSS EXAMINATION

MR. CLARK:

Q: Mr. Baggett, my name is Bob Clark, and I would

like to ask you a couple of questions, if I could, please, Sir. I noticed you had a video on. The video—was the car, did it cross the center line after you turned the video camera on?

A: No, Sir, it was before. We were sitting stationary, and observed it cross the line. Whenever we turned our overhead lights on, the camera comes on automatically.

Q: Okay. There were two officers in the car?

A: Yes, Sir.

Q: And, you pulled this car over, there were two black males in the car?

A: Yes, Sir.

Q: Then you went up, asked the driver to get out, and come to the back of the car.

A: Yes, Sir.

Q: You talked to the driver while the other officer went up and talked to the passenger?

A: Yes, Sir.

Q: There's a purpose in that, isn't there?

A: I'm not getting . . .

Q: Well, you separated them, and started talking to them together, didn't you?

A: Yes, Sir.

Q: Then, you and the other officer went back and compared what they said, didn't you?

A: Yes, Sir.

Q: That's when you decided to arrest them, didn't you?

A: No, Sir.

Q: Isn't that called profiling, Officer? Two black men in a car—you separate them, and talk to them?

MS. DOW: Object, Your Honor. Relevance . . .

THE COURT: Overruled.

Q: Isn't that what you call profiling?

A: No, Sir.

Q: You don't call that profiling?

A: No, Sir.

Q: Well, then, what do you call it when you stop black individuals, separate them, then talk to them for no traffic purpose, at all? What do you call that?

A: Checking the condition of the driver.

Q: Isn't it also called in your business, profiling?

A: No, Sir.

Q: Have you ever heard of profiling?

A: Yes, Sir.

Q: What's profiling?

A: It's whenever you specify one specific person, and pull them over continuously.

Q: Well, not just one person, but one race or one nationality, isn't it?

A: Yes, Sir.

Q: And, the real reason you pulled these guys over is because they were black, wasn't it?

A: No, Sir.

MR. CLARK: That's all. Thank you.

THE COURT: Any redirect?

MS. DOW:

Q: Where was the Jetta when you first saw it? How far away from your vehicle was it?

A: I'd say maybe thirty feet.

Q: Could you see who the driver of the vehicle was?

A: No, Ma'am. The windows were tinted on the vehicle.

Q: So you didn't know if the driver of the vehicle were black or white?

A: No, Ma'am.

Q: Did you observe the crossing of the line?

A: Yes, Ma'am.

Q: When there are two officers at a traffic stop, is there a concern for officer safety?

A: Yes, Ma'am. Trooper Rorman's main duty whenever he's—I guess you would call it a referred partner, which means he's on the passenger side. His main responsibility is to check for my safety. He has a better view into the vehicle to look for weapons, any open alcoholic beverages, anything of that sort. He can also look behind, and look for oncoming traffic.

Q: So, the officer looks into the vehicle and speaks to

the passenger to assist you and your safety—is that correct?

A: Yes, Ma'am.

Q: Did you stop the vehicle because you thought the driver might be intoxicated?

A: That is a concern of ours. That's one of the big—that's one of the things we have. Whenever people cross the center line, they are either intoxicated or not paying attention to what they're doing. They're a traffic hazard.

Q: Did you think he might be a danger to others on the highway?

A: Yes, Ma'am.

MS. DOW: No further questions.

THE COURT: Trooper, that concludes your testimony. Before you leave the stand, let me explain this to you. Don't talk to any of the other witnesses about what you have testified about.

THE WITNESS: Yes, Sir.

THE COURT: Thank you.

THE COURT: Call your next witness.

MS. DOW: Andy Dunklin.

ANDY DUNKLIN

Q: Tell us your name.

A: Andy Dunklin.

Q: How are you employed?

A: I'm a sergeant with the Texas Department of Public Safety assigned to the narcotics service for East Texas.

Q: How long have you been employed with the Texas Department of Public Safety assigned to the narcotics service for East Texas?

A: Sixteen years.

Q: I want to call your attention to April 20th of 2000. Do you recall conducting an interview with Frank Freeman on that day?

A: I do.

Q: At approximately what time did the interview take place?

A: About six o'clock in the evening.

Q: Did you ask Mr. Freeman where he was on April 20th, prior to the traffic stop?

A: Yes.

MR. CLARK: Judge, we're going to object to anything Mr. Freeman said under 804(b)(2).

THE COURT: It's not that, for sure. If there's any other basis, I would like to hear it.

MS. DOW: Your Honor, the questions the government is asking are to explain the conduct of Officer Dunklin.

THE COURT: Alright. I'm going to allow for a limited purpose. Ladies and Gentlemen, this officer is to testify as to why he took the actions he took. Let me explain carefully, so you will understand. He's going to say Frank Freeman told him certain things—that would be hearsay. You are not to take what he said Mr. Freeman told him as being true or accurate. Only that he was told this, and he acted on it. It's important you understand the distinction.

Q: Did you ask Frank Freeman where he was on April the 20th, prior to the traffic stop?

A: Yes, I did.

Q: Did you ask Frank Freeman where he was going?

A: I did.

Q: Did you ask him to whom the contents of the trunk of his Jetta belonged?

A: I did.

MR. CLARK: Judge, now we object to that . . .

THE COURT: Overruled.

MR. CLARK: Yes, Sir.

MS. DOW:

Q: Did you ask him to allow those questions?

A: I did.

Q: Did you receive answers to all those questions?

A: I did.

Q: In total, how long did your interview with Frank Freeman last?

A: About thirty minutes.

Q: After asking your questions and getting your answers, what did you do?

A: I took the vehicle Frank Freeman was driving, Frank Freeman, and myself, and I contacted David Fagan who is an agent with the Alabama Bureau of Investigation. I met Agent Fagan along with other Alabama agents in Jackson, Mississippi.

Q: About what time did you meet?

A: About two o'clock the following morning.

Q: Prior to leaving the trooper station, did you unlock the trunk of the Jetta?

A: Yes, I did.

Q: What did you see in the trunk?

A: I saw two large, black trash bags.

Q: Did you open them?

A: No.

Q: Did you take them out?

A: No.

Q: Did you re-lock the trunk?

A: Yes, I did.

Q: And, you transported the Jetta, Frank Freeman, and the contents in the garbage bags to David Fagan in Jackson, Mississippi—is that correct?

A: That's correct.

MS. GRIFFIN: Your Honor, the government has no further questions of this witness.

MR. CLARK: No questions, Your Honor.

RICHARD BRYARS

MS. GRIFFIN:

Q: Tell us your name, please, Sir.

A: Officer Richard Bryars.

Q: Can you spell your last name?

A: B-R-Y-A-R-S.

Q: How are you employed?

A: I'm employed with the Mobile Police Department, presently assigned to MCSENT drug task force.

Q: What does MCSENT stand for?

A: Mobile County Street Enforcement Narcotics Team.

Q: How many years of law enforcement experience do you have?

A: Over six years.

Q: Officer Bryars, I want to direct your attention to Friday, April the 21st of 2000. Did you assist in an investigation that afternoon?

A: Yes, Ma'am.

Q: Where were you located about five-thirty or six o'clock?

A: I was in the parking lot of UPS on Wolf Ridge Road on surveillance at Woodland Apartment Complex.

Q: Who else was located there with you?

A: I was in the vehicle with a Deputy Bryan Hill, and there were other members of MCSENT—Sergeant Mike Patterson, Rodney Patrick, and Deputy Anthony Gardner. And, other agents were out there . . .

Q: Why were you there?

A: We were there as a government surveillance team for a take down we were supposed to do at the apartment we identified as Frank Freeman's apartment.

Q: Were you in a position where you could see that apartment?

A: Yes, Ma'am—from the parking lot of UPS. Yes, Ma'am.

Q: Now, at that time, five-thirty or six on April 21st, it was still daylight—is that right?

A: Yes, Ma'am.

Q: Officer Bryars, was there a vehicle parked outside Frank Freeman's residence?

A: Yes, Ma'am.

Q: What type of vehicle was that?

A: That was a gold Volkswagon Jetta.

Q: Mr. Bryars, while you were there, did you see Sherman Williams?

A: Yes, Ma'am.

Q: How is it that you saw him?

A: Deputy Bryan Hill and I were on surveillance. We observed a black Toyota 4-Runner on Wolf Ridge Road going to the apartment. The car pulled into the parking lot of the complex, and it was driven by a female. The occupant got out of the vehicle, and we observed him and identified him to be Sherman Williams through photos I saw of him. He went to the area of Frank Freeman's apartment.

Q: Is Sherman Williams in the courtroom today?

A: Yes, Ma'am.

Q: Can you identify him?

A: Yes, Ma'am. He's sitting to the left of Mr. Clark in the gray suit.

Q: So, is this the individual you saw going to Frank Freeman's apartment on the late afternoon of April 21st of 2000?

A: Yes, Ma'am.

Q: Was is still daylight?

A: Yes, Ma'am.

Q: What happened to the 4-Runner after Sherman Williams went into the apartment?

A: It was there for just a few minutes, and then it left.

Q: Where was Sherman when the 4-Runner left?

A: I believed him to be in the apartment, but I didn't— he was not in the vehicle . . .

Q: Mr. Bryars, how long was Sherman Williams in that apartment before you saw him again?

A: He was there for some time. The next time I saw him, was when he got into the gold Volkswagon Jetta, and drove it from the apartment complex.

Q: Was he by himself?

A: Yes, Ma'am.

Q: When he got in the Jetta, did he have anything in his hand?

A: I could not see from where I was—I could see him get in the car.

Q: He left in the same Volkswagon you identified?

A: Yes, Ma'am.

Q: How long was he gone?

A: We actually followed him around. He was not gone more than fifteen or twenty minutes at the most. We followed him around Prichard, and he went to a gas station on Highway 45. He was there for a short time, and then returned to the apartment.

Q: What did he do at the gas station?

A: He parked the car and went inside. I couldn't see what he was doing inside, but, he came back out and he talked to a couple of people out by the gas pumps. Then, he got back in the car, and drove back to the apartment.

Q: Did he appear to go back in Frank Freeman's apartment?

A: Yes, Ma'am.

Q: During that time, was Frank Freeman still in the apartment?

A: Yes, Ma'am.

Q: Officer Bryars, how long was Sherman Williams in the apartment this time before you saw him again?

A: Just a matter of minutes.

Q: Did you see him leave the apartment?

A: Yes, Ma'am.

Q: By that time, was it becoming dark?

A: Yes, Ma'am.

Q: What did you see when he came out the second time from the apartment?

A: He was carrying some kind of object. I couldn't tell from the distance, but he was carrying some object toward the vehicle.

Q: What did you see happen?

A: At that time, I tried to get on the radio and advise the other units he was back outside. Before I knew it, that's when we were getting the word to do a take down.

Q: Did you see anybody with Sherman Williams when you got the word to do the take down?

A: No, Ma'am.

Q: Did you see the trunk of the Jetta had been opened?

A: Yes, Ma'am.

Q: What did you do when you got the word to do the take down?

A: Bryan Hill was driving the vehicle. We were the first vehicle in—we were suited up with our badges and jackets identifying ourselves as police. When we pulled into the parking lot, Mr. Williams was standing at the rear of the Volkswagon Jetta. And, as soon as—it appeared to me as soon as we pulled into the parking lot and I opened the door, he saw who we were. He took a defensive stance—or, kind of like a flight stance—then turned like he was getting ready to run. As I identified myself as a police officer, he turned the corner of the apartment complex and I was right behind him. He just took off running.

Q: You were dressed and identified yourself as police?

A: Yes, Ma'am.

Q: Raid jackets that said police?

A: Yes, Ma'am.

Q: You tried to stop him by saying you were the police?

A: Yes, Ma'am.

Q: He did not—he ran?

A: Yes, Ma'am.

Q: Did you see anything happen while he was running?

A: Yes, Ma'am. As soon as he turned the corner of the apartment complex, there were two air conditioning units on the side. I saw his hand go like this (indicating) as if he were throwing something down. I saw an object come out of his hand—I didn't know what it was at that point, but I continued the foot pursuit.

Q: You continued to pursue him?

A: Yes, Ma'am.

Q: How far did he run?

A: He ran all the way back up to Wolf Ridge Road where he was apprehended at the edge of a ditch by other officers on Wolf Ridge Road.

Q: There's a wire of some type just before the ditch—a power pole?

A: Yes, Ma'am.

Q: Now, could you show us where you saw him when you told him to stop, and where you were able to apprehend him?

A: You want me to get up?

Q: Please.

A: The vehicle was here, and it was backed in—he was standing about right here. We pulled in just short of where his vehicle was parked, and he was standing right here.

Q: Speak up.

A: He was standing right here. When I got out, he was already turning like he was fixing to run, and he had something in his hand. I said, "Police officer! Stop! Don't run!" The first thing he did was turn around, and cut the corner of the building. I was behind him at that point, and he threw it down—like that (gestures)—and came here to the back of the complex. He ran pretty much along the fence line until he got about right here where this power pole is and— that's where the ditch is—and, it was at the ditch where he was apprehended. At the ditch.

Q: In fact, did you think he tripped on the pole when he went into the ditch?

A: Yes, Ma'am. It's a deep ditch.

Q: So, you're saying he ran the distance all the way

behind the apartment in an attempt to go toward the road?

A: Yes, Ma'am.

Q: About how far would you say that was?

A: Maybe a hundred yards—maybe a little bit more.

Q: Was he finally stopped?

A: Yes, Ma'am.

Q: And, arrested?

A: Yes, Ma'am.

Q: Were you able to go back to retrieve what you saw him throw?

A: Yes, Ma'am.

Q: I show Government's Exhibit 18, and ask if you can identify it?

A: Yes, Ma'am. That was the two bags of suspected marijuana I found where he—I saw the object he threw down.

Q: This is what you retrieved?

A: Yes, Ma'am.

Q: Are they in the plastic bag on the back of Government's Exhibit 18?

A: Yes, Ma'am.

Q: Now, Officer Bryars—were those drugs sent to the laboratory? The marijuana?

A: Yes, Ma'am.

Q: Well, did the lab return it to be marijuana?

A: Yes, Ma'am.

Q: Did you go back to the location the next day when it was daylight?

A: Yes, Ma'am, I did.

Q: Did you find anything else?

A: Yes, Ma'am. We were looking for the key to the Volkswagon Jetta. We searched the area, and I backtracked to where Mr. Williams ran. I located the key next to the power pole by the ditch.

Q: The power pole close to Wolf Ridge Road where you identified he went into the ditch?

A: Yes, Ma'am.

Q: Is that where you found the key?

A: Yes, Ma'am.

MS. GRIFFIN:

Q: Officer Bryars, after Sherman Williams was arrested on the night of the 21st, was it dark by that time?

A: Yes, Ma'am, very dark.

Q: After he was arrested, did the officers go back to the Volkswagon Jetta parked outside Frank Freeman's apartment?

A: Yes, Ma'am.

Q: What did you retrieve?

A: Since we did not have the key to open the trunk, the door was open and the back seat could be laid down. There were two very large garbage bags in the trunk of the vehicle that contained bags of suspected marijuana.

Q: Why couldn't you open the vehicle at that time? Right after Sherman Williams arrest?

A: Well, we did not have the key to the vehicle.

MS. GRIFFIN: That's all we have at this time of this witness.

THE COURT: Cross-examination.

MR. CLARK:

Q: Officer Bryars, how are you this morning?

A: Pretty good.

Q: You said you set up surveillance at the Woodlands Apartments.

A: Yes, Sir.

Q: You say Sherman Williams came out twice—once when he went to the service station and drove around in Prichard, and the second time is when he was arrested.

A: Yes, Sir.

Q: Those are the only two times you saw him out of the apartment?

A: Yes, Sir.

Q: Alright. The second time he came out of the

apartment, did you see Frank Freeman with him?

A: No, Sir.

Q: The entire time you were there, Frank Freeman didn't come out?

A: Not that I saw, Sir.

Q: Not that you saw—he could have come out, but you just didn't see him.

A: Yes, Sir.

Q: But, none of the times Sherman came out of the apartment did you see Frank Freeman with him?

A: No, Sir.

Q: Now, did you—when he came out of the apartment, did you see anything in his hand?

A: No, Sir. Not from the angle I was at.

Q: It was dark, wasn't it?

A: Yes, Sir. At some point it was. Yes, Sir . . .

Q: At the point where you start to proceed up to the Jetta—up to the back of the Jetta—it was pretty dark at that time, wasn't it?

A: Yes, Sir. It was already dark.

Q: And, as you got there, Sherman was just standing at the back of the Jetta?

A: Yes, Sir.

Q: And, he had a couple of packages in his hand, I believe you said.

A: Yes, Sir.

Q: You can tell that's one of these small little bags, I think, that have been introduced?

A: Yes, Sir.

Q: At that time, you were dressed in civilian clothing, except you had a jacket on . . .

A: Yes, Sir.

Q: The front of the jacket doesn't say police, does it?

A: Yes, Sir.

Q: It has a badge. It just has a badge on it, doesn't it?

A: It's got a badge on it, also, that says police on it.

Q: Okay. Did you have your weapon drawn?

A: No, Sir.

Q: Did you have anything in your hand?

A: My radio.

Q: Alright. Now, you come up to the back of the car, and that's when—it's dark at that time, isn't it?

A: Yes, Sir.

Q: And, that's over on Wolf Ridge Road?

A: Yes, Sir.

Q: Mr. Williams started running around the building?

A: Yes, Sir.

MR. CLARK: Okay. I think that's all. Thank you, Sir.

THE COURT: Any redirect?

REDIRECT EXAMINATION

MS. GRIFFIN:

Q: Officer Bryars, how large is the word police on the front of the jacket?

A: It's a four-inch by two-inch patch that has a black background with gold lettering.

Q: When Sherman Williams continued to run, did you continue to identify yourself as police?

A: Yes, Ma'am.

Q: Were there other policemen there dressed and identified as policemen, as well?

MR. CLARK: Judge, could I have just one question? I hate to do . . .

THE COURT: Do it from there . . .

RECROSS EXAMINATION

MR. CLARK:

Q: Okay. There weren't any uniformed officers out there, were there?

A: We did have Mobile County Sheriff's Office out there with the K-9 unit, I believe—and, they were uniformed.

Q: But, at the time he started running, there were no uniformed officers present, were there?

A: On Wolf Ridge Road, yes, Sir. There was not in the apartment complex.

MR. CLARK: That's all. Thank you.

THE COURT: Any follow-up, Ms. Griffin?

MS. GRIFFIN: No, Sir.

THE COURT: Your next witness, Ms. Dow?

MS. GRIFFIN: David Fagan.

THE COURT: If you will, come on up and be sworn in, please.

DAVID FAGAN

MS. DOW:

Q: Tell us your name.

A: My name is David Fagan.

Q: How are you employed?

A: I am employed as an agent with the Alabama Bureau of Investigation. I'm currently assigned to the Drug Enforcement Administration.

Q: How long have you been employed in that capacity?

A: I have been with the State of Alabama for over ten years, and I have been with the DEA about two-and-a-half years.

Q: On the evening of April the 21st—April the 20th—did you receive information from agents in Texas concerning an arrest that had been made during a traffic stop?

A: Yes, Ma'am, I did.

Q: And, based on that information, what did you do?

A: I contacted agents—my supervisors at ABI and at DEA—and I advised them agents in Texas had an individual who was willing to cooperate and make a controlled delivery of approximately fifty pounds of marijuana.

Q: On that evening, did you speak to Andy Dunklin?

A: Yes. I did.

Q: After learning the information from Andy Dunklin, what did you do?

A: Sargent Dunklin and I made arrangements to meet each other, along with other agents and the cooperating Defendant in Jackson, Mississippi.

Q: What happened when you met?

A: At that time, we—after the precursor introduction and such—we transferred custody of the individual being arrested, Frank Freeman, his vehicle, and fifty pounds of marijuana. They were transferred to the custody of me and Agent Tony Calderaro.

Q: Then what did you do?

A: We went back to Mobile, Alabama with all of this—with marijuana, Freeman, and his vehicle. We met at the DEA office. Other agents were called in, and we formulated a plan as to how we would get—set up surveillance at Freeman's apartment, and left from there.

Q: After forming your plan, did you go to Frank Freeman's apartment?

A: We did.

Q: Who went with you?

A: Myself, Agent Tony Calderaro, and Special Agent Dana Ridenour, along with Freeman went to his apartment. We set up video and audio surveillance equipment in Freeman's apartment, and made recorded phone calls to Williams from his apartment.

Q: What did you do with the marijuana?

A: The marijuana was brought from the—we drove that vehicle to Freeman's apartment.

Q: The Jetta, you mean?

A: Yes, Ma'am. We took the marijuana out of the vehicle, and placed it in the apartment with us where we could visually see it at all times.

Q: And, you said Frank Freeman made some phone calls, is that correct?

A: Yes, Ma'am, he did.

Q: Who did he call?

A: He called Sherman Williams.

Q: These calls were recorded, is that correct?

A: They were.

Q: In the apartment, audio and video equipment were set up while you were there?

A: Yes, Ma'am, that's correct.

Q: How long did you stay in the apartment?

A: I stayed there, I guess, until we determined Mr. Williams was still in Dallas, Texas, and he wouldn't be there for some time. I believe myself and Agent Calderaro left the apartment at approximately ten or eleven o'clock that morning.

Q: At that time, were other agents in the apartment?

A: That's correct. Agent Ridenour remained in the apartment—I don't recall exactly. I think Randy Paton and Kendrick Wright took our place in the apartment.

Q: Throughout the day, were you involved in surveillance of the exterior of the apartment?

A: Yes, Ma'am.

Q: Did there come a time when Sherman Williams came to Frank Freeman's apartment?

A: Yes, Ma'am.

Q: Approximately, when did he come?

A: I believe it was approximately five P.M. that afternoon.

Q: After arriving, did there come a time when you saw him leave?

A: Yes, Ma'am. I believe on two occasions Williams left the apartment in the Jetta. One occasion he just drove around as if he were trying to pick up or identify any surveillance in the area. The second occasion, he went to a convenience store nearby, went inside, then made several phone calls on a pay phone outside.

Q: Around 8:30 P.M., what did you do?

A: So, at that time, Williams and Freeman took the marijuana that was in the house out to the Jetta, and Williams placed the marijuana in the trunk of the Jetta.

Q: And . . . excuse me. Go ahead . . .

A: At that time, the take down signal—the arrest signal—was given, and we attempted to arrest Williams. He subsequently fled when the agents identified themselves.

Q: Who put the marijuana in the trunk of the Jetta?

A: Sherman Williams.

Q: Do you see the person in the courtroom today who put the marijuana in the trunk of the Jetta?

A: Yes, Ma'am.

Q: Could you identify him, please?

A: At the table over there, sitting next to Mr. Clark.

Q: After Sherman Williams was arrested, did you assist in processing Mr. Williams into custody?

A: Yes, Ma'am, I did.

Q: And, did you take—as part of that processing, did you take custody of his wallet?

A: Yes, Ma'am, I did.

Q: Did you go back to search the Jetta that night?

A: Yes, Ma'am.

Q: Can you identify Government's Exhibit 19?

A: Yes, Ma'am. Theses were items that were taken out of the Jetta that were seized—that Freeman had been driving when he was arrested.

Q: On the 21st, you searched the vehicle, and you also obtained custody of the wallet of Sherman Williams, is that correct?

A: Yes, Ma'am.

Q: I want to show you what has been marked as Government's Exhibit 24(a). Can you identify Exhibit 24(a)?

A: That's the marijuana that was seized out of the two garbage bags that were taken out of the Volkswagon Jetta.

Q: On the 21st, after Sherman Williams placed the marijuana in the Volkswagon Jetta, did it come into your custody from the Volkswagon Jetta? And, when did it come into your custody?

A: That night, the marijuana was taken from the scene and locked up at Alabama Bureau of Investigations, our office there. It was placed there until Monday morning. Myself and Agent Calderaro took the marijuana to the DEA office, and we processed it for analysis to be shipped to the DEA south central lab.

Q: Was it sent to the lab for analysis?

A: Yes, it was.

Q: Have you received the results of that analysis?

A: I have.

Q: What was that result?

A: The contents of the Ziplock baggie was, in fact, marijuana.

Q: It was approximately fifty pounds of marijuana—is

that correct?

A: I believe it was closer to forty-four pounds, or somewhere around there. Yes, Ma'am . . . total.

Q: Can you identify Government's Exhibit 24(c), please?

A: This would be some marijuana. Following Williams's arrest, a consent search was done at his apartment off Grelot Road. This is the marijuana found in the residence, and the bag underneath it was the bag it was originally packaged in when it was found.

Q: Have you sent this exhibit to the lab for analysis?

A: Yes, Ma'am.

Q: What was the result?

A: It was marijuana.

Q: When did this come into your custody?

A: On the 21st.

Q: You said you thought the weight of the marijuana in the box was approximately forty-four pounds. Would you read the exact weight, please, from the crime lab report?

A: Yes. The net weight submitted to the laboratory was 21.48 kilograms.

Q: What was the exact weight of Government's Exhibit 24(c), the marijuana on the table taken from Frank Freeman's apartment?

A: Approximately 21.3 grams—just shy a couple of grams from an ounce.

Q: Were you aware when Sherman Williams was

running from the apartment? Did you observe him running from the apartment?

A: Yes, I did.

Q: At that time, were there blue lights activated?

A: Yes.

Q: Were there officers in the parking lot?

A: Yes, Ma'am.

Q: Can you identify Government's Exhibit 18, please?

A: I believe this was the marijuana that was thrown by Williams as he ran, and later recovered by Richard Bryars.

Q: Was Government's Exhibit 18 sent to the lab?

A: Yes, Ma'am, it was.

Q: Was it determined to be marijuana?

A: It was.

Q: What was the weight of Government's Exhibit 18?

A: Approximately 100.3 grams of marijuana.

Q: The following Monday after the arrest of Sherman Williams, did you view the video tape made on the day of his arrest?

A: Yes. Ma'am.

Q: After viewing the video tape, did you the later speak with Frank Freeman concerning a black bag?

A: Yes, Ma'am.

Q: Why did you speak to Frank Freeman?

A: Because we noticed in the video tape that Williams entered the apartment with a black bag in his hand. After the arrest and all the other evidence was gathered out of Freeman's apartment, we realized the black bag had not been retrieved.

Q: Is this the black bag that had been entered into evidence as Government's Exhibit 5?

A: Yes, it is.

Q: So—you went back and spoke to Freeman about the black bag. For what purpose?

A: We wanted to know where the black bag was, and to see if there were anything else in the bag.

Q: Did you ask him about the contents of the bag?

A: We did.

Q: Did you take the bag into custody at that time?

A: Yes, Ma'am—shortly after that, we did.

Q: What was in the bag?

A: There were some personal items. Clothing items, toiletry items, and approximately twenty-four thousand dollars in cash, I believe.

Q: Did there come a time when you came to believe there may have been more currency in the black bag?

A: Yes, Ma'am.

Q: When was that?

A: I believe that was during Mr. Williams's detention hearing.

Q: What did you do in response?

A: We brought Frank Freeman back into the office, and questioned him about the bag again—we asked if there had been more money in that bag than what we took out.

Q: What did he tell you?

A: He stated yes, there was, and he took . . . he was not sure how much money he took out. Several thousand dollars, maybe . . .

Q: What did you do in response?

A: We contacted the U.S. Attorney's office, and a complaint was drawn up for Mr. Freeman.

Q: In addition to the currency and clothing items in the bag, was there also a cellular phone in the bag?

A: Yes, Ma'am.

Q: In addition to the marijuana Sherman Williams placed in the trunk of the Jetta, the marijuana which Sherman Williams threw on the ground, and the marijuana which had been placed on the table in Frank Freeman's apartment, was there score marijuana also? Was the apartment Sherman Williams occupied with Tasma Scott searched?

A: Yes, Ma'am.

Q: When was it searched?

A: That same night following this arrest.

Q: Was marijuana also found in that apartment?

A: Yes, Ma'am.

Q: And, did you send that marijuana off for analysis?

A: Yes, Ma'am.

Q: What were the results of the analysis?

A: It was marijuana.

Q: Could you tell me the exact quantity of marijuana found in the Grelot Road apartment?

A: Yes, Ma'am—approximately 11.6 grams of marijuana.

MS. DOW: The government has no further questions.

CROSS EXAMINATION

MR. CLARK:

Q: Good morning, Officer Fagan. How are you this morning?

A: Good morning, Sir. Fine, thank you.

Q: So—you were out at the Woodland Apartments in surveillance, is that correct?

A: Yes, Sir.

Q: Did you know where Officer Bryars was at that time?

A: Yes, Sir—in the UPS parking lot across the street.

Q: Bryars was?

A: I believe so, yes, Sir.

Q: Where were you?

A: Well, at different times of the day, I was in the apartment for several hours, and then after Williams arrived, of course, I left and did not go back to the apartment. I was across the street at a business a couple of blocks away.

Q: Who had the best surveillance—you, or Bryars?

A: Bryars, and the people in the apartment.

Q: Okay. And, who was the first officer there at the Jetta that evening?

A: I believe it was Richard Bryars, but I don't know for sure.

Q: Okay. He had the best view of the apartment and the car, did he not?

A: From the outside.

Q: Yes, Sir—from outside. And, he pulled up there first, got out of his car, and approached Mr. Williams, did he not?

A: Yes, Sir.

Q: At the time you heard about the take down and Richard Bryars was the first to approach, where were you?

A: I was at the entrance of the parking lot coming into—

Q: Do you mind showing? Do you mind stepping down, please, and showing us where you were?

A: I had been in this area here (indicating). We were coming into the parking lot. Richard Bryars was already out of the vehicle . . .

Q: Where was your car, originally—where Mr. Bryars' car was, and the back of the Jetta?

A: Yes, Sir. Okay—parked somewhere in this area here (indicating).

Q: So, he had somewhat of almost a straight shot across to see, is that right?

A: Yes, Sir.

Q: You could not see Sherman when he came out of the house, could you?

A: No, Sir.

Q: Alright. But, Bryars was the one who went up first. He saw whatever he saw and, as a result of what he saw, he took off up there.

A: Yes, Sir.

Q: Okay. So, you did not see Sherman come out of the apartment.

A: No, Sir.

Q: Bryars did that?

A: Yes, Sir.

Q: Okay. So you did not see Sherman come out of the apartment, and you didn't see him start to run. You saw him as you came down this way, is that right?

A: Yes, Sir.

Q: The first time you saw him was when he was coming down by the fence, is that right?

A: Yes, Sir.

Q: You didn't see him take anything out of the apartment, did you?

A: I did not.

Q: You didn't see him put anything in the trunk of the car, did you?

A: I did not.

Q: You didn't see him throw anything on the ground, did you?

A: I did not.

Q: Okay. Now, then apart from Grelot, had you ever been to that apartment before?

A: No, Sir, I had not.

Q: Okay—had you ever seen Sherman Williams at that apartment?

A: No, Sir.

Q: So, you don't know whether Sherman ever stayed there or not?

A: I had never seen him at that apartment, no, Sir.

Q: And, you know the apartment was registered in someone else's name, wasn't it?

A: Yes, Sir.

Q: Ms. Tasma Scott, is that correct?

A: That's correct.

Q: You can't say to this jury, under oath, whether Sherman Williams was ever in that apartment or not, can you?

A: No, Sir. I never saw him there. I can't say that.

Q: With regard to Frank Freeman, you went out to

Freeman's house and the money was not in the bag, was it?

A: No, Sir.

Q: He had the money hidden, didn't he? Correction—the money was in the bag, just not all of what you thought was in there . . .

A: Oh, your client . . .

Q: Well, let me ask you this—the first time you went out there, did he have the money in the bag or not?

A: The first time?

Q: Yes, Sir.

A: After Williams was arrested—is that what you're referring to?

Q: Yes, Sir. The first time you went out and got the bag—saw the bag—was the money in the bag?

A: You know, I do believe it was, but I'm not positive.

Q: Do you recall going to get the money off the hot water heater?

A: The bag was back behind the hot water heater.

Q: But, was the money on top of the hot water heater?

A: I don't recall.

Q: Did Mr. Freeman tell you at that time he took a hundred and fifty dollars of the money to buy some tires?

A: Yes, Sir.

Q: Later on, did you go back and confront Mr. Freeman again with regard to the money?

A: Yes, Sir.

Q: At that time, did he tell you he lied to you earlier?

A: About?

Q: Pardon?

A: About what?

Q: About the money. About the amount of money.

A: Yes, Sir.

Q: He told you he lied to you?

A: Yes, Sir.

Q: And, that he took more than a hundred and fifty dollars?

A: That's correct.

Q: In fact, he told you he took between nine and ten thousand dollars, didn't he?

A: I believe that's correct.

Q: Up until that time, Mr. Freeman had not been arrested for anything, had he?

A: No, Sir.

Q: There were no federal drug charges pending against him, or anything pending against Mr. Freeman, were there?

A: I'm sorry?

Q: There were no charges, drug charges or any other kind of charges, pending against Mr. Freeman.

A: Well, he was going to be arrested for marijuana.

Q: Well, he was arrested on the 21st for marijuana, wasn't he?

A: No, Sir, he was not. He was not placed under arrest.

Q: And, he was not arrested on May 21st for marijuana, was he?

A: That's correct.

Q: He was not arrested for anything until you found out he lied about the ten thousand dollars—is that correct?

A: That's correct.

Q: After the ten thousand—that's when he got arrested for everything.

A: He got arrested. Yes, Sir.

Q: Did you stand out in the hall and have a conversation with officer Dunklin?

A: I did.

Q: Were you talking with Agent Dunklin about the case?

A: No, Sir.

Q: Just discussing the weather?

A: Discussing taking him to the airport as soon as I got off the stand. That kind of thing . . .

MR. CLARK: Thank you, Sir. No further questions . . .

THE COURT: That concludes your testimony.

(RECESS)

THE COURT: Alright, Ms. Griffin.

MS GRIFFIN: We call John Wall.

THE COURT: Sir, just come right up here by the court reporter and be sworn in, please.

JOHN WALL

MS. GRIFFIN: Tell us your name, please, Sir.

A: John Wall.

Q: Mr. Wall, how are you employed?

A: I own an automobile dealership in Mobile.

Q: Where is it located?

A: Tillman's Corner.

Q: Is that at Highway 90?

A: Uh-huh.

Q: Mr. Wall, do you know Sherman Williams?

A: Yes, I do.

Q: How do you know him?

A: He purchased an automobile from me.

Q: What type automobile?

A: It was a Volkswagon Jetta.

Q: Is Mr. Williams in the courtroom today?

A: Yes.

Q: Could you tell us what he's wearing?

A: A gray suit.

Q: When did Mr. Williams purchase a car from you?

A: I did not bring my records with me. I don't remember. It was sometime last year, or this year.

Q: Who made the down payment on the car?

A: Mr. Williams.

Q: Mr. Williams physically came to the business?

A: Yes.

Q: Do you recall in whose name the vehicle was placed?

A: It was placed in the name of Roderick Ward.

Q: Who told you to put it in that name?

A: Mr. Williams.

Q: Mr. Wall, did there come a time when you repossessed that Volkswagon Jetta?

A: Yes, I did.

Q: Why did you do that?

A: Non-payment.

Q: Non-payment for the note?

A: That's right.

Q: Did Mr. Williams later come to try to retrieve that car?

A: Yes, he did.

Q: What do you mean by 'retrieve' a car that's been repossessed?

A: Well, in this case I required him to pay the balance in full, plus the cost involved in repossessing it.

Q: So, he would have to pay the note off, and your visit of repossession?

A: Yes.

Q: Did Sherman Williams do that?

A: Yes, he did.

Q: Did he come into your business to do that?

A: Yes, he did.

Q: Was he by himself?

A: No.

Q: Who was with him?

A: I didn't get all of their names—Mr. Ward was with him when he picked it up the last time. There were several people with him, but I didn't get any of the names.

Q: Mr. Ward, Mr. Williams, and some other individuals?

A: Yes.

Q: Were they males?

A: Yes, I believe so.

Q: What happened when Mr. Williams came in?

A: Well, I gave him a receipt for the money, signed off

the release of the lien on the title, and surrendered the car to him.

Q: How much did Mr. Williams pay for the car the day he retrieved it after repossession?

A: He came in twice. He came in and brought me, I think, three or four hundred dollars one week—then, about ten days later, he brought the rest of it.

Q: Approximately what was the balance?

A: Seems like it was around twelve hundred dollars.

Q: Did he bring that in United States currency, in cash?

A: Yes, it was cash.

Q: These are the business records you maintained about that Volkswagon Jetta?

A: Yes.

Q: Can you tell us by looking at the documents the date the vehicle was purchased? Do you need your glasses?

A: Yes, I do. Okay—this was on November 19th, 1999.

Q: Is there anything on the paperwork that shows Sherman Williams's name?

A: No.

Q: At whose request was that?

A: That was Mr. Williams's request.

MS. GRIFFIN: Thank you, Sir. That's all we have of this witness.

THE COURT: Alright.

CROSS EXAMINATION

MR. CLARK:

Q: Mr. Wall, my name is Bob Clark. I don't think we've met before, have we?

A: Just by telephone several years ago.

Q: Okay. I won't ask what that was about. Did you know Mr. Williams? Well, let me ask you this . . . when was the first time you met Mr. Williams?

A: The day he came on the lot looking for an automobile.

Q: And, you never saw him before?

A: No, Sir.

Q: The day he came on the lot—was that the 19th of November?

A: It could have been the 18th. It took us a couple of days to get it worked out.

Q: At the time he came on the lot, was anyone with him?

A: Yes, Sir. There were people with him every time he came on the lot.

Q: Mr. Ward was with him, is that correct?

A: Yes, Sir.

Q: Was Mr. Williams driving his own vehicle?

A: Yes, Sir. As I recall, it was a late model, black sport utility vehicle.

Q: A 4-Runner?

A: Yes.

Q: Mr. Ward agreed to purchase the car, did he not?

A: Yes, Sir.

Q: And, he asked you to put it in his name?

A: Uh-huh.

Q: He's the one who gave you the money for the car, wasn't he?

A: No, Sir.

Q: Who gave you the money?

A: Mr. Williams.

Q: Did he count it out to you?

A: Yes, Sir.

Q: Was it your understanding the car was purchased, regardless of who paid for it, was being purchased for Mr. Ward?

A: That was intimated, yes.

Q: But, Mr. Ward needed a car, and that why they were buying that car?

A: I guess.

Q: Well, you knew Mr. Williams pulled up in a car and he had a car, didn't he?

A: Yes, he did.

Q: Mr. Ward didn't.

A: That's right.

Q: They told you that.

A: As far as I know . . . I don't know if he didn't have a car.

Q: All the documents were in Mr. Ward's name, were they not?

A: That's correct.

Q: How much was paid down on the car?

A: Four thousand dollars.

Q: How much was the total purchase price?

A: I think I was asking forty-nine eight-eight for the car, and taxes and everything brought it up to around fifty-two or fifty-three hundred. But, I don't have the papers in front of me. I'm just going from memory.

Q: Okay. Now, there's four thousand down, so that left about a twelve hundred dollar balance.

A: Approximately.

Q: Sometime after this, there was four hundred paid, then there was nine hundred laid.

A: I'm sorry?

Q: After the car was purchased . . .

A: Uh-huh.

Q: There was one payment of four hundred dollars.

A: Not until I repossessed it—there was nothing paid.

Q: Oh, they never made a payment.

A: Never made a payment.

Q: Okay. But there was a four hundred dollar payment and, I believe, there was a nine hundred dollar payment.

A: It was in two groups of money. I don't remember the exact dollar amounts—but, he came in and paid a lot of it. He asked me to hold it another ten days or so, and I did—then he brought in the rest of it.

Q: Mr. Ward was with him?

A: Mr. Ward was with him when he picked it up the last time. When he came in and laid the first amount of money, I'm not sure if he was with him or not. But, when the car was picked up, I requested Mr. Ward be there because the title was in Mr. Ward's name.

Q: Right. So, you signed off on the title, and Mr. Ward drove off in the car?

A: I don't know who drove off in the car—I got my money. That's all I wanted.

Q: I understand. But, you didn't know if Mr. Ward was there at the time.

A: He was there when it was picked up the final time.

Q: Okay. And, the car . . . then they left. Is that right?

A: Yes, Sir.

MR. CLARK: Thank you.

THE COURT: Mr. Wall, that concludes your testimony.

MS. DOW: Greg Soltis.

THE COURT: Alright. Mr. Soltis, if you would, come on

up to be sworn in.

GREG SOLTIS

MS. DOW:

Q: State your name.

A: Greg Soltis.

Q: By whom are you employed?

A: By the Drug Enforcement Administration, South Central Laboratory.

Q: Where are your official headquarters?

A: In Dallas, Texas.

Q: What is your official title?

A: I'm a fingerprint specialist.

Q: What are your duties?

A: Included among my official duties are the examination of various types of evidence associated with narcotic offenses for the presence of latent prints. These items of evidence include, but are not limited to tapes, plastic packages, plastic bags, and paper items.

Q: How long have you been employed in fingerprint work?

A: Over eighteen years.

Q: Have you had specialized training in the science of fingerprint scanner?

A: I have.

Q: Are you a member of any professional organizations dealing with the science of fingerprints?

A: Yes. I am a member of the International Association for Identification.

Q: Is that known as I.A.I.?

A: It is.

Q: Okay—does the I.A.I certify persons as latent print examiners?

A: Yes.

Q: I'm going to show you what's been marked as Government's Exhibit 24(b). Have you seen Government's Exhibit 24(b) before?

A: I have.

Q: Where did you see Government's Exhibit 24(b)?

A: In my office at the South Central Laboratory in Dallas, Texas.

Q: Did you examine 24(b) for latent prints?

A: Yes.

Q: What was the result of this examination?

A: I was able to develop and photograph two hundred and one latent fingerprints on the various plastic bags. I believe fifty-six plastic bags were contained within Government's Exhibit 24(b)

Q: Did you mark on each item where you located that latent print?

A: Yes.

Q: I'm going to show you what has been marked as Government's Exhibit 23. Can you identify it for us, please?

A: I can.

Q: What is Government's Exhibit 23?

A: Government's Exhibit Number 23 is a standard fingerprint card bearing the known ink fingerprints of one, Sherman Cedric Williams.

Q: Did you examine Exhibit 18 for latent prints?

A: Yes.

Q: What was the result of this examination?

A: I concluded two of the latent prints contained on the plastic bag were made by the Defendant, Sherman Williams.

THE COURT: Alright. Thank you, Sir.

MS DOW: The government has no further questions of this witness.

CROSS EXAMINATION

MR. CLARK: Mr. Soltis, my name is Bob Clark. I would like to ask you a few question, please.

A: Yes, Sir.

Q: Fingerprints is not an exact science, is it?

A: I'm sorry?

Q: It's just your opinion, isn't it?

A: Fingerprint identification is an exact science. It is the strongest means of personal identification recognized by the court system in this country, and the world.

Q: Sir, what you have told us here today is simply your opinion, isn't it?

A: That's correct.

Q: It's not—there no scientific formula or mathematical formula—that you can say this is certainty, is there? Is there?

A: There is no mathematical formula. However, if you are referring to statistical analysis that has been conducted in the area of fingerprint science, that study has been conducted. Yes, Sir.

Q: But, what we are talking about is not mathematical certainty or any kind of certainty. What we're talking about is your subjective opinion, isn't it?

A: We are talking about opinion testimony.

Q: Your subjective opinion, isn't it? Do you know the difference between objective opinion and subjective opinion?

A: No, Sir—it is objective opinion if the characteristics of the two prints were not within the confines I previously described to the jury, then I would not have effected an identification.

Q: I know. But, you're the one calling the shots, aren't you? This is not anything you put in a machine or anything like—you just look at it through your eyeballs, and say they look like the same to me, don't you? Don't you?

A: That's correct.

Q: There nothing scientific about it. You simply look at it and say, yes, in my opinion that's that, don't you?

A: I disagree. It is scientific.

Q: Do you do anything, but look at it with the eyeballs?

A: No.

Q: So you're just looking at it, and forming an opinion based on what you see, aren't you?

A: That's correct.

Q: Now, with regard to making matches, there is a minimum number of identifications you have to make a match, isn't there?

A: No.

Q: Are you familiar with the FBI manual on fingerprint analysis?

A: I am.

Q: Does that manual state there has to be a minimum of seven matches before you can call on it?

A: I believe you are misinformed, Counselor. There is no set number of characteristics needed for an identification.

Q: So, what you're saying is if you just have one whorl, you can say that's a match.

A: There are many, many characteristics contained within that whorl you describe.

Q: Sir, I'm talking about . . .

A: Yes—a fingerprint pattern within itself can contain anywhere between seventy-five to over one hundred and fifty individual characteristics.

Q: Have you ever made a mistake, Sir?

A: The policy as presented by the FBI the standards is each identification rests on its own merits. It's based upon the number of characteristics, the clarity of the fingerprints, and the overall uniqueness of those characteristics in and of themselves.

Q: Have you ever made a mistake, Sir?

A: Not in regard to fingerprint identification.

Q: So, as a human being and making these judgment calls, you have been perfect?

A: In my identification of unknown latent fingerprints to the known fingerprints of individuals, I have never made an erroneous identification.

Q: So you've been perfect?

A: If that's the term that you want to call me, I appreciate it. Yes, Sir.

Q: Okay. You've been perfect with regard to these analyses, even though they are just your opinion.

A: Yes.

MR. CLARK: Thank you.

THE COURT: Alright. Your next witness.

MS. GRIFFIN: We call Demetrius Thomas.

THE COURT: Come on up and be sworn in, Mr. Thomas. Just step right over here by the court reporter for a minute, please, Sir.

DEMETRIUS THOMAS

MS. GRIFFIN: Tell us your name, please.

A: Demetrius Thomas.

Q: Mr. Thomas, are you currently a federal prisoner?

A: Yes, Ma'am.

Q: How old are you?

A: Twenty-four.

Q: Mr. Thomas, did you enter a guilty plea to conspiracy to possess with intent to distribute marijuana?

A: Yes.

Q: As part of that agreement, did you agree to provide substantial assistance to the United States?

A: Yes.

Q: Are you doing that in hopes of receiving a lighter sentence?

A: Yes.

Q: Have you been promised any particular sentence?

A: No, Ma'am.

Q: Do you understand who will determine the sentence you receive?

A: Yes, Ma'am.

Q: Mr. Thomas, before your arrest, where were you living?

A: Wesley Avenue.

Q: Was there a time when you lived with Demetrius Sanders?

A: Yes, Ma'am.

Q: Who was Demetrius Sanders?

A: Just a friend of mine.

Q: Did you live with Demetrius Sanders at some time?

A: Yes, Ma'am.

Q: Where was that?

A: Wesley Avenue. Eastwood Apartments.

Q: Who paid for that apartment?

A: I don't know who paid for the apartment.

Q: Did you pay for it?

A: No, Ma'am.

Q: Did Demetrius Sanders pay for it?

A: No, Ma'am.

Q: Who told you that you could live in that apartment?

A: Sherman said it was alright.

Q: Sherman who?

A: Williams.

Q: Is he in the courtroom today?

A: Yes, Ma'am.

Q: Could you point him out for us?

A: Right over there in the gray suit next to Mr. Clark.

Q: How did you meet Sherman Williams?

A: In the studio.

Q: What studio?

A: Shake 20.

Q: Where is that located?

A: In Prichard.

Q: Do you know the street it's on?

A: On Love Joy Loop, or something like that.

Q: Love Joy Loop in Prichard?

A: Yes.

Q: How is it that you met Sherman Williams at Shake 20?

A: Just being up there with my cousin. He just came up sometimes.

Q: Who was your cousin?

A: Jerrel Simon.

Q: Mr. Thomas, did there come a time you knew anything about marijuana connected with Sherman Williams?

A: Not at the time. Not when I was just coming up there.

Q: Did there come a time when you learned something about marijuana and Sherman Williams?

A: Yes, Ma'am.

Q: Approximately when was that?

A: I would say about March, or February.

Q: Of what year?

A: '99.

Q: 1999. How did you learn something about marijuana connected with a Sherman Williams?

A: I took a trip with Roderick Ward.

Q: Who is Roderick Ward?

A: A friend of Sherman's.

Q: Where did you and Roderick Ward take a trip to?

A: Texas.

Q: How did you get there?

A: Drove Sherman's Grand Marquis.

Q: Who asked you to go to Texas?

A: Sherman and Ward.

Q: Sherman Williams and Roderick Ward?

A: Yes, Ma'am.

Q: Did you know what you were going to Texas for?

A: Not at the time.

Q: Did you agree to go to Texas?

A: Yes, Ma'am.

Q: What did you do when you got there?

A: When we got there we waited for a while, and we picked up the marijuana and came back home.

Q: Now, you said that was sometime in 1999?

A: Yes, Ma'am.

Q: Do you know the exact month?

A: No, Ma'am, I don't know the exact month.

Q: When you were in Texas, where did you and Roderick Ward go?

A: A friend named Dee—to Dee's apartment

Q: Who introduced you to Dee?

A: Well, it was just me and Roderick, so he introduced me to her.

Q: What happened at Dee's apartment?

A: Well, we counted—we went there, and counted money. And, you know, picked up marijuana and came home.

Q: How much marijuana did you receive?

A: Something like a hundred pounds.

Q: How do you know how much it was?

A: Roderick told me.

Q: Did you see the marijuana?

A: No, I saw the container it was in.

Q: What kind of container was it?

A: A trash bag.

Q: A black trash bag?

A: Yes.

Q: How did the marijuana get to Dee's apartment?

A: I don't know how. When we got there, I guess it was already there.

Q: Did you see any money change hands?

A: Yes, Ma'am.

Q: Could you tell us about that? Can you sit up so we can hear?

A: Yes, Ma'am.

Q: Could you tell us about the money you saw change hands?

A: Well, first of all, when I counted some of the money—most of the money—then Ward exchanged with the other guy.

Q: There was a man at Dee's apartment?

A: Yes.

Q: Did you know who he was?

A: No.

Q: What happened to the money?

A: He took the money and left.

Q: How much money was it?

A: I don't know exactly how much, but I just counted

like thirty thousand, thirty-five—something like that.

Q: Was it United States currency?

A: Yes, Ma'am.

Q: Who gave you and Roderick Ward that thirty-something thousand dollars?

A: Sherman.

Q: When did he give it to you?

A: The night we left.

Q: From where?

A: We was at some hotel. I don't know, some hotel. I don't know the name of it.

Q: In Dallas or Mobile?

A: In Mobile.

Q: So you had the money before you went to Texas?

A: Yes, Ma'am.

Q: After you and Roderick paid the man for the marijuana, what happened to the marijuana?

A: We loaded it into the car, and we left.

Q: You left. Had you seen Sherman Williams in Dallas on that trip?

A: No, Ma'am.

Q: What did you and Roderick Ward do with the hundred pounds of marijuana?

A: Drove it back to the apartment.

Q: You drove it back. What happened then?

A: Then he took me home.

Q: Who took you home?

A: Roderick.

Q: Do you know what happened to the hundred pounds of marijuana?

A: No, Ma'am.

Q: Mr. Thomas, did there come a time when you were asked to make another trip to Dallas, Texas?

A: Yes, Ma'am.

Q: After the first trip, about how many weeks passed before you made a second trip?

A: I don't know exactly how much time, but it was not too far.

Q: Several weeks?

A: Yes, Ma'am.

Q: Who asked you to make the second trip?

A: Sanders came to me and asked me the second time.

Q: Who is Sanders?

A: Demetrius Sanders.

Q: That was your roommate?

A: Yes, Ma'am.

Q: What did you agree to?

A: Drive back out to Texas, and pick up some more.

Q: What did you drive to Texas?

A: The Grand Marquis.

Q: The same Marquis?

A: Yes, Ma'am.

Q: Who gave you the vehicle?

A: Sherman gave us the car.

Q: Did you take any money to Texas?

A: No, not then. Just gas money, and stuff like that.

Q: Who gave you gas money?

A: Sherman.

Q: Sherman Williams?

A: Yes, Ma'am.

Q: Mr. Thomas, where did you and Demetrius Sanders go in Texas?

A: Back to Dee's apartment.

Q: Who came to that apartment?

A: Sherman came later.

Q: Sherman Williams?

A: Yes, Ma'am.

Q: But, he didn't drive to Texas with you and Demetrius Sanders?

A: No, Ma'am.

Q: Do you know how he got from Mobile to Dallas, Texas?

A: I think he flew.

Q: What did you base that opinion on?

A: Because one time we had to pick him up from the airport.

Q: Mr. Thomas, what happened when Sherman came to Dee's apartment?

A: Well, he came and just met the guy, met the guys that were there who we was waiting on. We made the deal, and we left.

Q: Was this a man who came to Dee's apartment?

A: Yes, Ma'am.

Q: Did he bring marijuana?

A: Yes, Ma'am.

Q: Was he paid for the marijuana?

A: Sherman paid him.

Q: How much marijuana was there?

A: The second time, like, 50 pounds.

Q: How was it wrapped? What did it come in?

A: It was just like they had been—in the bags, but the bag was sealed over.

Q: What type of bag?

A: The trash bag.

Q: How was the marijuana packaged within the trash bag?

A: Sometimes it was like just a block.

Q: Do you know how many pounds each block weighed?

A: No, it was, like, one block.

Q: The entire thing was a block. What happened with that marijuana?

A: We broke it down, and weighed it up.

Q: Who broke it down, and weighed it up?

A: Sherman.

Q: Who was present?

B: Me and Sanders.

Q: And, Sherman Williams?

A: And, Dee.

Q: Was the man still there who brought the marijuana?

A: Yes, Ma'am.

Q: Do you know who he was?

A: No, Ma'am.

Q: After Sherman weighed and broke it up, what happened to the marijuana?

A: We loaded it into the car, and we left.

Q: Who left?

A: Me and Sanders.

Q: Okay—where was Sherman when you and Demetrius Sanders left?

A: Still in the apartment.

Q: Did you bring that marijuana back to Mobile?

A: Yes, Ma'am.

Q: What happened to it?

A: Waited at the studio for Sherman to come.

Q: At Shake 20?

A: Yes, Ma'am.

Q: In Mobile?

A: Yes, Ma'am.

Q: Do you know how he got from Dallas to Mobile?

A: No, I don't know how he got back.

Q: What happened with the marijuana once Sherman Williams came to Shake 20?

A: He took it.

Q: He took the marijuana. Were you paid for these trips?

A: Well, the money to get back home with . . .

Q: But, you didn't make a profit from it?

A: No, Ma'am.

Q: Mr. Thomas, did there came a time when you made a third trip to Texas for Sherman Williams?

A: Yes, Ma'am.

Q: Approximately, when was that?

A: A few weeks—almost a month.

Q: So, later '99, early 2000?

A: No, it was still '99.

Q: Late '99—is that right?

A: Yes, Ma'am.

Q: I want to direct your attention to March the 2nd of 2000. Were you driving a Mercury Marquis on that day?

A: Yes, Ma'am.

Q: Who was with you?

A: Me and Demetrius Sanders.

Q: Whose vehicle was that?

A: Sherman's.

Q: How do you know?

A: Well, he said it was his.

Q: Did he give you that vehicle?

A: Yes, Ma'am.

Q: Were you stopped in that vehicle?

A: Yes, Ma'am.

Q: Where?

A: In Saraland.

Q: Who was with you?

A: Me and Demetrius Sanders.

Q: Can you describe the car for me?

A: Just a tan Marquis.

Q: Was your car searched at the time of your stop?

A: Yes, Ma'am.

Q: What was found inside the vehicle?

A: Three pounds of marijuana, and a handgun.

Q: Three pounds of marijuana, and a handgun—whose marijuana was that?

A: Well, Sherman gave it to Sanders, and he was going to drop him off, but we never made it.

Q: You were dropping Sanders off with the marijuana. Where was the marijuana in the vehicle?

A: In the trunk.

Q: Whose gun was it?

A: I don't know.

Q: Was it yours?

A: No, Ma'am.

Q: Did you see the gun when the officers got it from the vehicle?

A: Yes, Ma'am.

Q: Did you know the gun was in the vehicle?

A: Yeah, I knew it was in there.

Q: How did you know that?

A: It was in the glove compartment at first, and Demetrius Sanders took it out.

Q: Where did Demetrius Sanders put it?

A: Under the seat.

Q: Was the handgun in the car when you got it from Sherman Williams?

A: Yes, Ma'am. I didn't look in the glove compartment when we first got it, but it was in the car we found it a little while later.

Q: You didn't see anybody put it in there after you got the car from Sherman Williams, did you?

A: No, Ma'am.

Q: Were you taken to the Saraland Police Department?

A: No, Ma'am.

Q: After the stop, you were not taken to the Saraland Police Department?

A: No, Ma'am.

Q: Were you questioned by Dana Ridenour with the FBI?

A: Yes, Ma'am.

Q: Don't tell us what you told them, but did you tell her where you got the marijuana?

A: Did I tell her where I got the marijuana?

Q: Did you tell the officers when Ms. Ridenour came where you got that marijuana?

A: No, I didn't tell them a thing when they stopped me.

Q: No, Sir. Do you remember talking to Ms. Ridenour?

A: Yes, Ma'am.

Q: Did you tell her where you got the marijuana?

A: Yes, Ma'am.

Q: Mr. Thomas, after the date you were stopped with the three pounds of marijuana and a gun with Demetrius Sanders, did you make another trip for Sherman Williams to Texas?

A: I made one more.

Q: One more trip. Was that in early April?

A: Yes, Ma'am.

Q: Where did you go?

A: Back to Texas.

Q: Why did you go back to Texas?

A: To pick up marijuana.

Q: Who asked you to go?

A: Sherman.

Q: Did you transport any money?

A: No, Ma'am.

Q: How did you go to Texas?

A: A Crown Victoria.

Q: Whose car was that?

A: Bobby Rander.

Q: Who gave you that vehicle?

A: Sherman had given it to me.

Q: Was Sherman dating Bobby Rander's sister, Nikki Rander?

A: Yes, Ma'am.

Q: And, he gave you the Crown Vic that belonged to Bobby Rander?

A: Yes, Ma'am.

Q: Who went to Texas with you?

A: Shanera Colston.

Q: Where did you go in Texas?

A: To Dee's apartment.

Q: Did you check into a hotel on this occasion?

A: Yes, Ma'am. I checked into a hotel.

Q: Do you remember where the hotel—the name of the hotel?

A: The Ramada, and the Holiday Inn—and, I think, the Royal Inn, or something like that.

Q: Why did you go to so many different hotels?

A: They were different days.

Q: You stayed more than one day?

A: Yes, Ma'am.

Q: Who paid for—who gave you the money for the hotels?

A: He had just gave me money to . . . for going, but I spent it.

Q: Who gave you the money?

A: Sherman.

Q: While you were on this trip three days, did you go to Dee's apartment?

A: Yes, Ma'am.

Q: What happened at Dee's apartment?

A: We had to go pick Sherman up from the airport.

Q: Who did?

A: Me, Dee, and Shanera.

Q: Once you picked Sherman up, where did he come from?

A: Mobile.

Q: Where did you go with Sherman Williams?

A: We went back to Dee's apartment.

Q: What happened at Dee's apartment?

A: Well, that night nothing happened. We just spent the night. We went back over there the next day.

Q: On April 4th, what happened?

A: We picked up the marijuana.

Q: How did you pick up the marijuana?

A: Some other guy brought it over.

Q: Was it the same guy you had previously seen?

A: Yes, Ma'am.

Q: What was the marijuana contained in?

A: A bag.

Q: What type of bag?

A: A trash bag.

Q: A black trash bag?

A: Yes, Ma'am.

Q: How much of the marijuana was brought to Dee's apartment on that day?

A: Fifty pounds.

Q: Who paid for the marijuana?

A: Sherman did.

Q: Mr. Thomas, again, did Sherman Williams examine the bags of marijuana?

A: Yes, Ma'am.

Q: What happened after Sherman Williams paid for that marijuana?

A: I was on my way home, and got stopped.

Q: Did you get stopped by a Texas Trooper?

A: Yes, Ma'am.

Q: Were you headed to Mobile, Alabama?

A: Yes, Ma'am.

Q: About how far from Dallas, Texas were you?

A: I really don't know how far.

Q: Well, how long had you been gone from Dee's. Apartment?

A: About thirty minutes.

Q: Where was the marijuana?

A: In the back seat.

Q: What happened when you were stopped?

A: I was searched.

Q: Was the marijuana discovered and seized?

A: Yes, Ma'am.

Q: Were you arrested?

A: Yes, Ma'am.

Q: Have you been in jail since April the 4th?

A: Yes, Ma'am.

Q: So, Mr. Thomas, altogether, how many trips did you make to Texas for Sherman Williams?

A: It was five.

Q: Mr. Thomas, when you were going to Dallas, Texas, in late 1999, was Sherman Williams employed with the Dallas

Cowboys?

A: I don't believe so.

Q: You did not know him to have a job at that time, did you?

A: No, Ma'am.

Q: Did you know in the past he played football for the Dallas Cowboys?

A: Yes, Ma'am.

MS. GRIFFIN: That's all I have at this time.

THE COURT: Alright. Let's break for lunch before we start cross examination.

THE CLERK: We have been advised by his attorney, Brad Lee Murray, that Mr. Rice intends to take the fifth, and thus we will not call him. We would like to put him on record that he intends to follow the advise of his counsel.

THE COURT: And, you are satisfied he has a privilege that would be violated if he were asked questions and answered them?

MS. GRIFFIN: I am satisfied if he answered truthfully he would incriminate himself.

MR. MURRAY: I would advise him to assert his Fifth Amendment right not to testify, Judge.

THE COURT: Well, do we need to put anything else on record?

MS. GRIFFIN: I would like for Mr. Rice to state his name and that he intends to follow the advise of his counsel.

THE COURT: Alright. Mr. Rice, tell us your full name, please, Sir.

MR. RICE: Kenneth Lamar Rice.

THE COURT: Alright. Now, if you were called to the stand in this case and asked by the government's attorney certain questions regarding dealing . . .

MS. GRIFFIN: Only regarding his involvement with Sherman Williams . . .

THE COURT: Yes—your involvement with Sherman Williams, insofar as certain alleged marijuana transactions, would you take the Fifth Amendment, and ask that you be protected from testifying?

MR. RICE: Yes, Sir.

THE COURT: And, you would refuse to testify?

MR. RICE: Yes, Sir.

MS. GRIFFIN: And, as to cocaine, Your Honor . . .

THE COURT: Alright. That clears that up. Thank you.

MR. MURRAY: Thank you, Judge.

THE COURT: Alright, then. Which, Mr. Clark, in my judgment, prohibits either party from commenting on the witnesses not being here, and not being called.

MR. CLARK: Yes, Sir, Judge. I'm not going to . . .

THE COURT: Okay. We are ready for your next witness, Ms. Griffin.

THE COURT: Alright. Ladies and Gentlemen, everybody get comfortable now, and we will continue . . .

DAY 2, PART 2

DECEMBER 5, 2000

DEMETRIUS THOMAS

THE COURT: The witness having been previously sworn to tell the truth, the whole truth, and nothing but the truth, returned to the stand, was examined, and testified as follows:

MR. CLARK:

Q: Mr. Thomas, my name is Bob Clark. I don't think we have ever met before, have we?

A: Yes, Sir.

Q: Okay. I won't ask you anymore. Here's a copy of your plea agreement. Let me ask you to look at it to see if you, in fact, actually signed that agreement, and if that is your plea agreement with the government.

A: (No audible response.)

Q: Let me put this on it. Okay. I'm going to ask you some questions about that in just a second, so you'll have it in front of you. You have not been sentenced at this time, have you?

A: No, Sir.

Q: Your sentencing came up on a prior occasion, but it was continued, wasn't it?

A: Yes, Sir.

Q: It was continued until you could testify—is that right?

A: Yes, Sir.

Q: Your testimony—you were told your testimony was going to be needed, and your sentence would be withheld until such time as you testified. Is that right?

A: Yes, Sir.

Q: Alright. Now, your plea agreement there, Sir, on page three, I believe, of your plea agreement. It talks about substantial assistance, is that correct? The first paragraph talking about that you will provide the government with substantial assistance.

A: Yes, Sir.

Q: And, you had a lawyer at the time you signed this, did you not?

A: Yes, Sir.

Q: And, you fully understood what everyone was talking

about, did you not?

A: Yes, Sir.

Q: Now, prior to signing this agreement, you went to a probation conference where it was explained to you what your sentence would be, wasn't it?

A: Not exactly what my sentence would be, but I talked to the probation people.

Q: Okay. They filled out some forms, and told you what your sentence . . . the range of punishment. Is that right?

A: Yes, Sir.

Q: You knew the range of punishment under your indictment was five to forty years, didn't you?

A: Yes, Sir.

Q: And, you told the government you would provide substantial assistance, didn't you?

A: Yes, Sir.

Q: That was more than just providing assistance. It was providing substantial assistance, wasn't it?

A: Yes, Sir.

Q: And, substantial assistance meant the more people you got involved, the better you did for the government—the better the government would do for you, wasn't it?

A: I don't think . . . I don't remember that part there.

Q: Well, were you told the government would make a recommendation for you?

A: Well, no. Not exactly . . .

Q: Well, exactly read your plea agreement. Does the plea agreement say exactly the government will make an exact recommendation for you?

THE COURT: Do you have the paragraph?

MR. CLARK:

Q: It's the second paragraph on page three. We're on page three. It's the second paragraph down. Do you see there where it says the government will recommend a sentence of twenty-three months?

A: Yes, Sir.

Q: So, they did make an agreement with you, didn't they?

A: Well, not the government.

Q: Does it say there the government will recommend a sentence of twenty-three months?

A: Yeah. That's what they say. It was read to me by my lawyer.

Q: Pardon.

A: It was read to me by my lawyer.

Q: So, your sentencing came up once before, but the government asked to put it off, didn't they?

A: Yes, Sir.

Q: Because you have not always been truthful with the government, have you?

A: What do you mean?

Q: Well, you lied to the government. In the past, Mr.

Thomas, you lied to the government, didn't you?

A: I don't know exactly what you're talking about.

Q: Okay. Do you recall on March the 2nd, or shortly after March the 2nd, when you were stopped in Saraland, you had a discussion with the FBI agent who's been sitting here? Ms. Ridenour is gone, but the little blonde FBI agent—I probably shouldn't say little blonde. But, the lady who's been sitting here—do you recall seeing her this morning?

A: Yes, Sir.

Q: Do you know Ms. Ridenour?

A: Yes, Sir.

Q: Did you have a conversation with Ms. Ridenour that you would tell her the truth, that you would cooperate with her?

A: Yes, Sir.

Q: That was your agreement with her, is that right?

A: Yes, Sir.

Q: And, in exchange for that, she agreed to let you stay out on bond. Stay free . . .

A: Yes, Sir.

Q: Is that correct? But you didn't abide by that, did you?

A: Yes.

Q: Well, did you take Bobby Rander's Crown Victoria, and go to Texas after March 2nd?

A: Yes. I went back.

Q: Did you tell Ms. Ridenour you were going to go back?

A: No, Sir.

Q: So, you were lying to her. When you told her you would cooperate with the government, that wasn't true, was it?

A: Yes. it was true, but I just didn't tell her I went back.

Q: You didn't tell her when you went back. You didn't tell her until you got arrested, did you?

A: Yes, Sir.

Q: But, you had an agreement with her to tell her what you were doing, and what you were about, didn't you?

A: Yes, Sir.

Q: But, you didn't honor that agreement, did you?

A: No, Sir.

Q: You lied to her.

A: Yes, Sir.

Q: Then you were caught out in Texas on March 2nd, weren't you?

A: Yes, Sir.

Q: Then you came back to Mobile—is that correct?

A: Yes, Sir.

Q: And, at that time, you were detained and kept in custody because the judge found out you lied to Ms. Ridenour, didn't he?

A: Yes, Sir.

Q: And, that's why you are in custody today, isn't it?

A: No, I don't think so.

Q: Well, didn't Judge Cassady sign a detention order? Do you remember going up to Judge Cassady on the third floor, and having a detention hearing?

A: I remember the judge, but I don't remember his name.

Q: Okay. Do you remember it being brought out to him you lied to Ms. Ridenour about going to Texas?

A: Yes, Sir.

Q: Have you seen this order signed by Judge Cassady? Do you have a copy of that order?

A: No, Sir.

Q: You have never seen that?

A: No, Sir.

Q: Your lawyer never showed that to you?

A: I don't remember. I don't remember. I don't recall.

Q: Okay. But, you do remember a hearing before Judge Cassady?

A: Yes, Sir.

Q: And, do you recall Judge Cassady—Ms. Ridenour said you had not been truthful with her?

A: Yes, Sir.

Q: After she said that, the judge detained you, didn't he?

A: Well, yes, Sir.

Q: You have been detained ever since, haven't you?

A: Yes, Sir.

Q: Now, you lived at the . . . was it Eastwick Apartments?

A: Yes, Sir.

Q: You lived there with Sanders—Demetrius Sanders.

A: Yes, Sir.

Q: He was living there before you got there?

A: Yes, Sir.

Q: You don't know whose name the apartment was in, do you?

A: No, Sir.

Q: You don't know who was paying the rent on it either, do you?

A: No, Sir.

Q: So, you met Sherman Williams somewhere around August of 1999, is that correct?

A: I knew him before that.

Q: Well, tell us when you met him.

A: It was in the early part of '99.

Q: Okay. Tell us about what month it was.

A: I don't recall the month.

Q: Was it spring? Was it in the winter? Spring? Summer?

A: I can't remember.

Q: Well, do you recall where you were when you met him?

A: Yeah. the studio.

Q: Pardon me?

A: The studio.

Q: Oh, the studio. That's Shake 20 here in Prichard—is that correct?

A: Yes, Sir.

Q: At that time, did you ask Mr. Williams for a job?

A: Well, no—he offered it to me.

Q: Okay. He offered you a job—is that correct?

A: Yes, Sir.

Q: The first job he offered you was to be security for a rap concert, wasn't it?

A: Yes, Sir.

Q: That was over in Mississippi, wasn't it?

A: Well, just security, period.

Q: I understand. But, the first job you worked on was a rap concert in Mississippi . . .

A: Yeah. But, they had their own security. I didn't do anything over there.

Q: That was the first job, and you went over there, wasn't it?

A: Yes, Sir.

Q: Do you recall a black college spring break, or something like that?

A: I don't know.

Q: Do you remember Gulfport, Mississippi?

A: Yeah, I remember.

Q: Okay. There were a lot of black college students there partying like a spring break type of deal, wasn't there?

A: I don't know. It was a club. I don't know whether it was spring break or not.

Q: Well, there were a lot of folks there . . .

A: Yeah. A lot of people.

Q: Colleges and places . . .

A: I don't know if it was a college or what—they was in a club.

Q: Did they appear to be college age students over in Gulfport ?

A: I don't know—I can't tell.

Q: Okay. You don't recall that being in August of 1999?

A: No. I don't recall what date.

Q: Well, what is your birthday, Mr. Thomas?

A: 5-14-76.

Q: Was it before or after your birthday you met Sherman Williams?

A: Which birthday?

Q: I'm sorry, the one you had in 1999—5-14-99.

A: No. I was locked up in '99.

Q: You were locked up in '99?

A: Yeah.

Q: Okay. On your birthday?

A: No. No. I wasn't locked up on my birthday.

Q: Okay—where were you in your birthday?

A: I don't know.

Q: Well, at the time, did you know Sherman Williams or not ?

A: Yeah, I knew him.

Q: You knew him. Had you been to Texas at that time?

A: Yeah—I had already been.

Q: That would have been somewhere around your birthday . . .

A: Before.

Q: Before your birthday. Okay. So, your first trip to Texas was before your birthday—is that right?

A: Right.

Q: That first trip before May, did you drive a Mercury Grand Marquis?

A: Yes, Sir.

Q: Do you know the owner of that vehicle?

A: They said it was Sherman's car. I don't know whose name it was in . . .

Q: Alright. Now, how many trips did you take out there? I think you told Ms. Griffin it was a couple of weeks later you went again in the Grand Marquis.

A: Yes, Sir.

Q: That would have been as late as June, or the first of July?

A: No. I don't recall the months, or the dates.

Q: Do you recall where Mr. Williams was working at that time?

A: No. I don't believe he was working.

Q: In the summer of 1999, did you know he was playing professional football for the Mobile Admirals?

A: Yeah—I knew he had started for the Admirals.

Q: Did you know he owned a studio called Shake 20 where he hired you to be security there?

A: Yes, Sir.

Q: Were you security there on numerous occasions?

A: Well, there was nothing going on—I was just there.

Q: You were getting salary, weren't you?

A: No, Sir—not for security.

Q: You just worked there for nothing. Now, the first two trips you say you took in the Mercury Marquis . . .

A: Yes, Sir.

Q: No question about it's being a Mercury Marquis?

A: No, Sir.

Q: Alright. And, the last trip you took, you took it in the Crown Victoria owned by Bobby Rander, didn't you?

A: Yes, Sir—the last trip.

Q: Okay. Working there at Shake 20, you had access to that Mercury Marquis, did you not?

A: Sometimes.

Q: It was basically a company car?

A: No, Sir.

Q: Was it parked there at the company?

A: No, Sir.

Q: Was it ever parked at the company?

A: If somebody was in it.

Q: Alright. Did you ever drive it by yourself?

A: Yeah, I drove it by myself before.

Q: Did you take it places on business?

A: No, Sir.

Q: You never took it on business. You just took it for personal pleasure?

A: Yes, Sir—whenever I used it in Alabama.

Q: And, then, you used it on numerous occasions, did

you not?

A: Well, a few times.

Q: Okay. Now, the drug dealings you had out in Texas was at Demetric Beans's house, weren't they? Is that what you told us?

A: Dee's apartment. I don't know the name . . .

Q: Okay. Dee's house. You identified the lady.

A: Yes, Sir.

Q: As Dee. And, you were there and picked up drugs.

A: Yes, Sir.

Q: Now, you told us the last time you got there, everything was there at the apartment, and you picked up drugs—is that right?

A: Which time are you referring to?

Q: The last time.

A: Yes, Sir.

Q: When you got arrested and got detained . . .

A: Yes, Sir. Wasn't nothing there when I first got there the last time.

Q: Okay. You say they came in the apartment. Somebody brought drugs in the apartment . . .

A: Yes, Sir.

Q: You took the drugs out, and put them in your car.

A: No, I didn't take them out, and put them in the car.

Q: Somebody else took them out, and put them in the car?

A: Yes, Sir.

Q: That was the fellow who brought the drugs there?

A: No, Sir.

Q: Who took the drugs out, and put them in the car?

A: Sherman put the drugs in the car.

Q: Sherman Williams put the drugs in the car?

A: Yes, Sir.

Q: Now, that was on the last occasion. That was when you were in the Crown Victoria, wasn't it?

A: Yes, Sir.

Q: You're sure it was Sherman who took that?

A: Yes, Sir.

Q: Now, did you ever see Roderick Ward with a gun?

A: No, Sir.

Q: You never knew Roderick Ward to carry a gun?

A: No, Sir. I didn't know him that well, but I never seen him with a gun.

Q: You never went to a pawn shop, bought a gun, and traded it with Mr. Ward?

A: No, Sir, I never bought anything from a pawn shop.

MR. CLARK: You never bought a gun from a pawn shop. Okay. Can I just have a second, Judge?

THE COURT: Yes, Sir.

MR. CLARK: That's all, Judge.

THE COURT: Okay, Mr. Thomas, that concludes your testimony.

THE COURT: Your next witness.

MS DOW: Trooper William Casper.

WILLIAM ERIC CASPER

The witness, after having been duly sworn to tell the truth, the whole truth and nothing but the truth, was examined and testified as follows:

MS. DOW:

Q: Tell us your name.

A: William Eric Casper.

Q: How are you employed?

A: By the Texas Department of Public Safety.

Q: How long have you been so employed?

A: Three and a half months. Correction. Three and half years.

Q: Were you working on April the 4th of 2000?

A: Yes, I was.

Q: On that date, did you notice a vehicle pulled off the roadway?

A: Yes, I did.

Q: Where did you notice the vehicle?

A: It was parked on the outside shoulder of I-29, 493 in Coffman County, Texas.

Q: Did you approach the vehicle?

A: Yes, I did.

Q: Why?

A: Because there was a driver outside the car. He had popped the hood, and he was apparently having some car trouble.

Q: Can you describe the vehicle?

A: Yes—it was a 1994 Crown Victoria. I believe it was a tan, gold-ish color.

Q: When you approached the driver standing outside the vehicle, what did you do?

A: I asked him if there were something wrong with his car, and he said yes. He said it overheating.

Q: Did you ask him for his identification?

A: Yes, I did.

Q: Who was the driver of the vehicle?

A: The driver did not have any identification on him, but he gave me the name of Demetrius Thomas.

Q: What was he doing when you approached?

A: He was working around the engine area compartment. He opened the radiator lid where you filled the radiator.

There was no steam coming from the engine. Also, he looked in the reservoir that held the windshield wiper cleaner. He then closed those, and closed the hood.

Q: Were you trying to see if you could offer him any assistance?

A: Yes, I was.

Q: Was anyone traveling with him?

A: Yes, there was.

Q: Who?

A: It was Shanera Colston, and she was sitting in the right front passenger seat.

Q: After observing the Defendant—I mean, Demetrius Thomas—working with his car, then what did you do?

A: I approached Shanera Colston, and asked if she could identify the driver. She identified him as Demetrius Thomas. I then asked her for an identification, and she gave me an AT&T calling card at that time. I then asked for another form of identification, and she presented me with an Alabama identification card identifying her as Shanera Colston.

Q: When you spoke with Shanera Colston, was she in the vehicle or outside the vehicle?

A: She was inside the vehicle. She had a blanket covering her.

Q: And, what did you do in response to seeing the blanket?

A: Okay. I told her to remove the blanket because I wanted to see her hands, and that was for my safety. At that time she gave me her identification.

Q: When she removed the blanket what did you see?

A: I saw evidence of marijuana usage in the form of blunt paper, and seeds on the floor.

Q: Did you make any other observations about the vehicle?

A: Yes, I did. I smelled a strong odor of marijuana emitting from the vehicle.

Q: What did you do then?

A: I then asked Mr. Thomas to step to the rear of the vehicle. I submitted all the information to DPS Dallas. Before I left the passenger side—or, the drivers side of the vehicle, I asked Ms. Colston specifically if there were any marijuana in the vehicle and she replied no.

Q: Then what did you do?

A: I submitted the information to DPS Dallas on the vehicle and both subjects. I then went back and asked Mr. Thomas about the marijuana smell that I was smelling from the vehicle. He then said that they had a package of blunts, but they had not yet opened it yet.

Q: And, did you ask for permission to search the vehicle?

A: Yes, I did.

Q: Was permission granted?

A: At first, he said the trunk, and then he said, "Well, she does have something in her purse," meaning marijuana cigarettes.

Q: Did you search the vehicle?

A: Yes, I did. For my safety, I told Ms. Colston to get

out of the vehicle, at which time there were twelve grams of marijuana that she was sitting on.

Q: Did you take her into custody?

A: Yes, I did.

Q: And, then proceeded to search the remainder of the vehicle?

A: Yes, I did.

Q: What did you find when you searched the vehicle?

A: I first searched the front passenger area. The only thing that was found was the twelve grams that Ms. Colston was sitting on. I then went to the rear passenger door, and there was a black Samsonite suitcase. I began to open the suitcase, at which time Ms. Colston approached the vehicle again and again, and wanted to talk. I told her to step to the rear of the vehicle, at which time I unzipped the suitcase and found a large sum of marijuana.

Q: Did you take the marijuana into your custody?

A: Yes, I did.

Q: Did you—what did do with it then?

A: It was locked at the DPS office into evidence, then it was transported the following day to the DPS lab in Garland, Texas.

Q: After locating the marijuana in the car, did you have occasion to take the Defendant, and the two individuals in the Crown Victoria into custody?

A: Yes, I did.

Q: In processing Demetrius Thomas into custody, did

you take some of the property he had on him?

A: Yes, I did.

Q: Can you identify Government's Exhibit 31?

A: Yes. These are the keys that came from their property.

Q: The property of Demetrius Thomas?

A: Yes.

MS. DOW: The government has no further questions.

MR. CLARK: No questions.

THE COURT: Alright, Trooper—that concludes your testimony.

RODERICK WARD

The witness, after having first been duly sworn to tell the truth, the whole truth, and nothing but the truth was examined and testify as follows:

MS. GRIFFIN:

Q: Tell us your name please, Sir.

A: Roderick Ward.

Q: Mr. Ward, do you have any nicknames or street names?

A: Yes, Ma'am.

Q: What are they?

A: Little Award and Juice.

Q: Mr. Ward, are you currently a federal prisoner?

A: Yes, Ma'am.

Q: Have you been charged as a co-defendant with Sherman Williams in a marijuana conspiracy?

A: Yes, Ma'am.

Q: In fact, did you enter a guilty plea to that charge?

A: Yes, Ma'am.

Q: Mr. Ward, have you also entered a guilty plea to passing counterfeit money?

A: Yes, Ma'am.

Q: As part of your current plea agreement, if you provide substantial assistance, do you hope to receive some reduction in your sentence?

A: Yes, Ma'am.

Q: Is what you are attempting to do today is provide substantial assistance?

A: Yes, Ma'am.

Q: Have you been promised any specific sentence?

A: No, Ma'am.

Q: Mr. Ward, are you currently awaiting sentencing on all of those charges?

A: Yes, Ma'am.

Q: Have you been promised any particular sentence?

A: No Ma'am.

Q: Do you understand that even if the United States asks for a reduction, it is entirely up to the judge as to whether you receive one?

A: Yes, Ma'am.

Q: Were you told by the court when you plead guilty that the court did not have to follow the plea agreement?

A: Yes, Ma'am.

Q: And, you persisted in your plea anyway, is that right?

A: Yes, Ma'am.

Q: Mr. Ward, have you previously been convicted of possession with the intent to distribute crack cocaine?

A: Yes, Ma'am.

Q: Was that in the early 1990s?

A: Yes, Ma'am.

Q: When did you get out on those charges?

A: 1996. And, I was released again. I violated, went back, and got released in 1997.

Q: Now, Mr. Ward, do you know Sherman Williams?

A: Yes, Ma'am.

Q: How do you know him?

A: He's a childhood friend.

Q: So you've known him how many years?

A: Since I was, maybe, twelve?

Q: Please tell us about your relationship with Sherman Williams.

A: Well, he's been my friend since we were, like, twelve years old.

Q: Is he in the courtroom today?

A: Yes, Ma'am.

Q: Could you point him out?

A: Yes, Ma'am.

Q: Tell us what he's wearing.

A: A gray suit.

Q: Does Mr. Williams own a business?

A: Yes, Ma'am.

Q: What type of business?

A: A recording studio.

Q: During your association with Sherman Williams, did you ever travel to Texas?

A: Yes, Ma'am.

Q: Why did you go to Texas?

A: When I first got out, I had a problem with snorting powder, and Mr. Williams tried to rehabilitate me.

Q: When you say snorting powder, you mean cocaine?

A: Yes, Ma'am.

Q: Mr. Williams took you to Texas with him?

A: Yes, Ma'am.

Q: What did you do there?

A: When I was in Texas, I stayed with him at his house.

Q: Where was that house? In Texas?

A: Yeah, in Texas.

Q: Dallas, or Fort Worth?

A: It was in Dallas.

Q: How long were you there with Mr. Williams?

A: He kept me at different periods of time.

Q: You would come back and forth to Mobile?

A: Yes, Ma'am.

Q: Now, at that time in '97, was Mr. Williams employed?

A: Ma'am?

Q: At that time, was Mr. Williams employed?

A: In 1997?

Q: Yes.

A: I didn't get out until '98.

Q: No—in '98 was he employed?

A: Yes, Ma'am.

Q: Who did he work for?

A: The Dallas Cowboys.

Q: Did there come a time when you made a drug trip to

Texas?

A: Yes, Ma'am.

Q: Did you learn about drugs while you were out there?

A: Yes, Ma'am.

Q: What happened?

A: Well, some guy kept calling. Mr. Williams owed him for some drugs. Sherman said he didn't owe him for no drugs.

Q: Wait a second—about when was that?

A: Sometime in '99.

Q: How did you get to Texas?

A: Mr. Williams took me.

Q: What happened while you were there?

A: A guy was calling, talking about . . .

Q: What, then, did Mr. Williams tell you about a phone conversation?

A: Well, he was saying that he didn't owe the guy no money for no drugs or nothing.

Q: What did you do?

A: I— then the guy was saying he owed him a thousand dollars. So, I got nine hundred dollars, and took it to him.

Q: Who did you get the nine hundred dollars from?

A: Mr. Williams.

Q: Why did you do that?

A: So we could pay the guy off. Go pay the guy . . .

Q: Did you pay the guy?

A: Yes, Ma'am.

Q: Do you know who he was?

A: It was a guy by the name of Dray.

Q: What did you give Dray?

A: I gave him nine hundred dollars, and told him from now on don't speak to Mr. Williams. From now on when he got anything to do with dope, do it through me.

Q: Why did you do that?

A: So no one could say they bought or sold any drugs from Mr. Williams.

Q: After you told that to Dray, what did you go back and tell Mr. Williams?

A: That from now on any illegal activity, I would be the one to handle it.

Q: Did there come a time during that same trip where you purchased marijuana from Dray for Sherman Williams?

A: Yes, I purchased from him.

Q: After you came from paying the nine hundred, how did it come to pass you purchased from him?

A: Then I went back to this guy Dray on three different occasions, and purchased ten pounds one each occasion.

Q: There were separate trips?

A: Yes, Ma'am.

Q: For a total of thirty pounds?

A: Yes, Ma'am.

Q: Of marijuana?

A: Yes, Ma'am.

Q: Who gave you the money to buy that marijuana?

A: Mr. Williams.

Q: Sherman Williams?

A: Yes, Ma'am.

Q: What did you pay for the ten pounds?

A: Thirty . . . thirty-five hundred dollars.

Q: Three thousand five hundred dollars?

A: Yes, Ma'am.

Q: What did you do with each of the ten pounds you got with the money from Sherman Williams?

A: I tracked the drugs, sold the drugs, and came back to Texas.

Q: When you say 'tracked the drugs,' did you bring them?

A: Yes, Ma'am, I did.

Q: From?

A: Texas.

Q: To where?

A: Mobile.

Q: Did you sell the ten pounds?

A: Yes, Ma'am, I did.

Q: How much did you make off the ten pounds of marijuana?

A: Eighty-five hundred.

Q: What did you do with the eighty-five hundred you made off each of the ten pounds?

A: Take it back to Texas.

Q: What did you do with it?

A: Give it to Williams.

Q: Now, after those trips, did there come a time when you and Mr. Williams had some distance between you?

A: Yes, Ma'am.

Q: Did you come back in his good graces and, at one point, make another trip?

A: Yes, Ma'am, I did.

Q: Approximately when was that?

A: Also in 1999.

Q: Who did you make that trip with?

A: Demetrius Thomas.

Q: What vehicle did you and Demetrius Thomas go in to Texas?

A: A gold Crown Victoria.

Q: Who gave you that vehicle?

A: Mr. Williams.

Q: What did you and Mr. Thomas take to Texas with you?

A: Money.

Q: Pardon?

A: Money.

Q: Who gave you the money?

A: Mr. Williams.

Q: Did you know how much it was?

A: I think sixteen thousand.

Q: What happened when you and Demetrius Thomas got to Texas?

A: We got a room.

Q: A hotel room?

A: Yes, Ma'am.

Q: Did anything happen in connection with drugs?

A: Yes, Ma'am.

Q: Tell us about that

A: Yes. Once I got there, I called Demetric Beans. Demetric Beans came from the hotel room that I purchased, and got the marijuana.

Q: Did Demetric Beans have a nickname?

A: Dee.

Q: What did she do?

A: She came to the motel and got me.

Q: Where did she take you?

A: To an apartment.

Q: She took you to her apartment?

A: Yes.

Q: What happened at the apartment?

A: It was a guy sitting there waiting on me. I purchased some marijuana.

Q: You purchased from him?

A: Yes, Ma'am.

Q: Did you give him the money you got from Sherman Williams?

A: Yes, Ma'am.

Q: How was the marijuana packaged?

A: It was packaged in baggies and a garbage bag.

Q: A black garbage bag?

A: Yes, Ma'am.

Q: What did you do with that marijuana?

A: I then tried to move it to Mobile.

Q: How did you get back to Mobile?

A: In the same car—the gold car.

Q: You and Demetrius Thomas?

A: Yes, Ma'am.

Q: And, what happened to the marijuana when you got back to Mobile?

A: I maintained the marijuana and, then, after a while, I received a call asking what I had did. At the time, I hadn't did much with the marijuana as far as selling the marijuana. So, I was told to give the marijuana to Demetrius Sanders.

Q: Who was Demetrius Sanders?

A: Ma'am?

Q: Who was Demetrius Sanders?

A: That's a friend of ours.

Q: Who told you to give the marijuana to Demetrius Sanders?

A: Sherman Williams.

Q: Did you do that?

A: Yes, Ma'am.

Q: Mr. Ward, you have seen Government's Exhibit 1, a Volkswagon Jetta.

A: Yes, Ma'am.

Q: Was that your vehicle?

A: No, Ma'am.

Q: Could you tell us about that vehicle?

A: Me and Mr. Williams went and bought the vehicle.

Q: Where did you buy it?

A: From a car lot on Highway 90—Package Low Price Auto.

Q: Do you know whether or not the vehicle was in your name?

A: Yes, Ma'am.

Q: Why was that?

A: At first, we had went and bought the vehicle and we really—you know, I was just driving the vehicle at first. And, then, after about a couple of weeks, we gave the vehicle to a female.

Q: You say we went and bought the vehicle. Who went and bought the vehicle?

A: Me and Mr. Williams.

Q: Why was it placed in your name?

A: I guess attention to that first.

MR CLARK: Judge . . .

THE COURT: You're getting a little close.

THE WITNESS: I guess attention, at first.

MR CLARK: Judge, I object to him guessing.

THE COURT: Yeah. Don't guess. Did somebody say that or not?

THE WITNESS: At first, the vehicle . . . we didn't say who the vehicle was going to be for. So, I took it by him telling me to sign my name the vehicle was going to be for me. But, I drive the vehicle maybe two or three weeks, and he took the vehicle from me. He come and got the vehicle, took the vehicle from me, and gave it to Ms. Anita Rander.

Q: Does she have a brother?

A: Yes.

Q: What is his name?

A: Bobby Rander.

Q: Is he also deceased?

A: Yes, Ma'am.

Q: Did he die in a drowning accident with Demetrius Sanders?

A: From what I read in the newspaper.

Q: Did you ever see that Jetta again after it was taken from you, and given to Anita Rander?

A: Yes, Ma'am.

Q: How did that happen?

A: I saw her driving it.

Q: Did you ever receive the vehicle back?

A: No, Ma'am.

Q: Did you ever pay anything for that vehicle?

A: No, Ma'am.

Q: Who paid for the vehicle?

A: Mr. Williams.

Q: Mr. Ward, are you familiar with another vehicle

connected with Sherman Williams?

A: Yes, Ma'am.

Q: Have you seen Government's Exhibit 25?

A: Yes, Ma'am.

Q: What type of vehicle is that?

A: A Crown Victoria, Grand Marquis. Grand Marquis.

Q: Who makes the Grand Marquis?

A: Mercury.

Q: How have you seen this vehicle, and where?

A: That's the vehicle I drove to Texas.

Q: You drove this vehicle to Texas?

A: Me and Demetrius.

Q: Who gave you this vehicle to drive?

A: Mr. Williams.

Q: This vehicle is not in your name, is it?

A: No, Ma'am.

Q: Have you seen Mr. Williams with a firearm?

A: Yes, Ma'am.

Q: Would you tell us if you recognize Government's Exhibit 27?

A: Yeah—that's Mr. Williams's nine millimeter.

Q: Who have you seen with this?

A: At first, I saw it with Mr. Williams, then Demetrius Thomas. He had it . . .

MS. GRIFFIN: That's all we have of this witness, at this time.

THE COURT: Alright. Mr. Clark.

MR. CLARK:

Q: Mr. Ward, my name is Bob Clark. I don't think we have met before, have we?

A: No, Sir.

Q: I would like to ask you a few questions, if I could, please, Sir.

A: Yes, Sir.

Q: When was the first time you went to—you were convicted of drugs and went of to prison?

A: The first time I was convicted in 1991.

Q: When did you get out of prison after 1991?

A: 1996.

Q: How long were you out before you were sent back?

A: Maybe six months.

Q: Okay. When did you get out the second time?

A: 1998.

Q: Do you recall about when?

A: Maybe February of '98.

Q: Okay. Now, then, you have known Mr. Williams since childhood, have you not?

A: Yes, Sir.

Q: When you got back in 1998, it was February. It was after the '97-'98 football season, wasn't it?

A: It could have been, Sir. I don't remember.

Q: Well, you got back in February. The '97-'98 football season ends in January with Super Bowl in January of '98, doesn't it?

A: Yes, Sir.

Q: So, when you got back, Mr. Williams had been through with football season?

A: He was working out.

Q: Right.

A: Yes.

Q: Did he have Shake 20 at that time?

A: Yes, Sir, he did.

Q: That's a recording studio, is it not?

A: Yes, Sir, it is.

Q: Out there in Prichard?

A: Yes, Sir, it is.

Q: They have recording equipment for people to come and . . . it's a music studio, isn't it?

A: It's a music studio.

Q: Right. And, they have a lot of rap artists, primarily, who go out there and make recordings, don't they?

A: Yes, Sir.

Q: Then other people sell those recordings, or take them to radio stations and try to get them played, don't they?

A: Yes.

Q: It's an attempt to distribute the music, isn't it?

A: Yes, Sir, it is.

Q: Did you ever go on the road and try to get radio stations to play and try to distribute the music?

A: No, Sir. I didn't.

Q: But Mr. Williams was. He was the owner of Shake 20, the music studio, wasn't he?

A: Yes, Sir, he was.

Q: Now, are you telling me you went to Texas the first time . . . you went to his house was in 1998, or was it? You tell me—I don't know.

A: I went in '98.

Q: Okay—can you tell us about what month you went in '98?

A: No, Sir, I can't.

Q: Well, was it summer, winter, fall?

A: It was sometime after I got out.

Q: Okay. You got out in February!

A: Yes, Sir.

Q: What's your birthday?

A: August.

Q: August?

A: August 31st.

Q: August 31st. Alright. Did you go there before your birthday?

A: I don't remember.

Q: Did you ever go out there while he was in training camp?

A: Yes, Sir.

Q: How long did you stay out there?

A: I guess I stayed out there a couple of weeks. It varied. Different times.

Q: Alright. Did you tell Mr. Williams you wanted to move to the Dallas area?

A: Yes, Sir.

Q: Did you ask him if you could stay at his house while you were contemplating moving to the Dallas area?

A: Yes, Sir.

Q: Did you have money of your own at that time?

A: No, Sir.

Q: You didn't have any money?

A: No, Sir.

Q: You got out there, and you were broke?

A: Yes, Sir.

Q: Alright. And, you stayed at Mr. Williams's house for a couple of weeks?

A: Yes, Sir.

Q: Did you look around to see if you wanted to live out in Texas?

A: Yes, Sir.

Q: Alright. And, all of this time, was Mr. Williams training for football?

A: Well, he was going and working out.

Q: Okay.

A: Yeah.

Q: At that time, you stayed two weeks and you came back to Mobile?

A: I stayed two weeks and different times like that . . .

Q: Okay.

A: Sometimes longer than two weeks.

Q: Alright. Mr. Williams was your host while you were in Texas?

A: Yes, Sir, he was.

Q: He provided you with a place to stay?

A: Yes, Sir, he did.

Q: You went out there on how many occasions?

A: Sir, I went out there on several different occasions.

Q: Okay. When you first started going out there, you went as a friend of Sherman Williams, and you were thinking about moving out there, weren't you?

A: Yes, Sir.

Q: Now, at some point in time, you met a lady by the name of Demetric Beans, did you not?

A: Yes, Sir.

Q: Alright. Did you ever have an occasion to send her money from Mobile?

A: No, Sir.

Q: By Western Union?

A: Not that I know—no, Sir.

Q: Well, let me show you. Maybe I can refresh your recollection. Let me show you . . .

MS. GRIFFIN: Mr. Clark . . .

MR. CLARK: This is it.

MS. GRIFFIN: I just want to see what you're showing him.

MR. CLARK:

Q: Let me show you a money gram, please, Sir. I'll ask you to look at it—see what it says there as the sender's name?

A: Roderick Ward.

Q: Okay. Did you send that money to Demetric Beans?

A: Sir, that's not my handwriting.

Q: Pardon?

A: That's not my handwriting.

Q: That's not your handwriting?

A: No.

Q: Okay. Now, when was the first time you claim you went out to Texas to pick up any drugs? Or, when did you pick up any drugs in Texas?

A: When I went to Texas to visit.

Q: Tell us when that was.

A: 1998, 1999, Sir.

Q: Okay. So, it was 1999 before you went and received any drugs?

A: Yes, Sir.

Q: At the time you went, where was Mr. Williams living?

A: He was living in his house.

Q: In his house?

A: Uh-huh.

Q: Did you know Mr. Williams rented his house in August of 1998?

A: No, Sir. I knew he was going to rent it. He was going to move out of his house.

Q: Yes, Sir.

A: But, I don't know in August of 1998 that he had already moved out.

Q: '98 was the last season that he was under contract, wasn't it?

A: Yes, Sir.

Q: At that time, when you were out there in the summer of'98, while he was in training camp, he told you he was going to move out of his house so he wouldn't be burdened with that after the'98 season, didn't he?

A: Said he was having a chance to go back with the Dallas Cowboys. They released him before, and called him back. There was a chance that Mr. Williams would play for the Cowboys team.

Q: His contract was '95,'96, '97 and '98—is that right?

A: To my knowledge, yes.

Q: Okay. And the contract went through the '98 season. They had to pay him for the '98 season?

A: Sir, they had also had released Mr. Williams. When they released Mr. Williams, they also called him back. And, as I recall, the running back was already hurt and they released him. So, therefore, Mr. Williams did have a chance to play again for the Dallas Cowboys.

Q: The first time you went out to Texas to buy any drugs you were in a gold Crown Victoria?

A: No, I was not. Not the first time I went out there.

Q: The second time?

A: The second time, no. Not the second time.

Q: When was it?

A: It was the fourth time.

Q: You took the Crown Victoria out there one time?

A: Yes, I did.

Q: Did you know Demetric Beans?

A: Yes, Sir.

Q: Have you been to her apartment?

A: Yes, Sir.

Q: Have you been to her apartment with Mr. Thomas?

A: Yes, Sir.

Q: So, have you even been to her apartment with Mr. Sanders?

A: No, Sir.

Q: How about Rander?

A: No, Sir.

Q: Have you been to her apartment when Frank Freeman was there?

A: No, Sir.

Q: Okay. Now when you first bought the Jetta, it was your belief the Jetta was your car, is that right?

A: Yes, Sir.

Q: Mr. Williams had a Toyota 4-Runner, did he not?

A: Yes, Sir.

Q: You made an agreement with the Government, did you not?

A: I plead guilty, yes, Sir.

Q: Okay. You had a lawyer at the time that you entered into your plea agreement, did you not?

A: Yes, Sir.

Q: And, your lawyer explained all of this to you, didn't he?

A: Yes, Sir.

Q: He told you there was a possibility you were going to be enhanced because of all your prior dealings?

A: Yes, Sir.

Q: You went to a probation conference with him where they explained all of this, didn't they?

A: Yes, Sir.

Q: How much time did they say you were going to get— statutory time for enhancement?

A: Twenty years.

Q: Twenty years. That was the minimum you could get, wasn't it?

A: Yes, Sir.

Q: You and your attorney agreed with the government not to file for any statutory enhancement, didn't you?

A: Yes, Sir.

Q: Which automatically puts you down under the

twenty years, doesn't it?

A: Yes, Sir.

Q: You told the government what you could help them with, didn't you?

A: Yes, Sir.

Q: The government told you what they could help you with?

A: It was a chance that I would get a reduction. They would not file for the enhancement.

Q: They would not file for the enhancement, number one?

A: Yes, Sir.

Q: So, you're down under the twenty now, aren't you?

A: Yes, Sir.

Q: Okay. You talked with your lawyer about what the government could do for you, didn't you?

A: Yes, Sir.

Q: Your lawyer told you the government was going to recommend about half of your sentence, the guidelines range, didn't he?

A: Yes, Sir.

Q: Tell the ladies and gentlemen of the jury what that amounts to . . .

A: Half my guidelines?

Q: Yes, Sir.

A: Four from fourteen, from eighteen to twenty-four months.

Q: Eighteen to twenty-four months. So, the government gave you eighteen years off of your sentence in order to get you to testify, didn't they?

A: They took . . . they wouldn't enhance me.

Q: Well, you have gone from a minimum of twenty years down to eighteen to twenty-four months, haven't you?

A: Yes, Sir.

Q: And, that's what you expect to get, don't you?

A: I'm hoping for a light sentence, Sir. They cannot guarantee it.

Q: I understand they can't guarantee it, but that's what they're going to recommend, isn't it?

A: I don't know—I'm not even sure what the government will recommend, Sir. I'm not going to speculate.

Q: Well, I know. But, you talked to your lawyer. Your lawyer was Ms. Cleveland, Ms. Lila Cleveland?

A: Yes, Sir.

Q: She explained all of this to you, didn't she?

A: Yes, Sir.

Q: And, you thoroughly understood it, didn't you?

A: Yes, Sir.

Q: This wasn't your first time to have a plea and do all of this, was it?

A: No.

Q: You've been down this road before, haven't you?

A: Have I plead guilty?

Q: Yes, Sir.

A: Yes, Sir, I have plead guilty before.

Q: Alright. Now—you agreed to tell the government in order to get your sentence reduced, and one of the things you had to do was provide substantial assistance, wasn't it?

A: Yes, Sir.

Q: That was more than just helping the government, wasn't it?

A: (No audible response)

Q: You had a discussion with Ms. Cleveland about what substantial assistance means. It means more than just assisting—it means substantial assistance.

A: It's doing . . . she explained to me that would mean what did I do.

Q: Uh-huh. What the government wanted you to say, is that right?

A: You say the government wanted me to say?

Q: Yes, Sir.

A: To cooperate?

Q: Yes, Sir.

A: Yes, Sir.

Q: Now—you agreed to take a polygraph in your plea agreement, didn't you?

A: Yes, Sir, I did.

Q: Did you ever take a polygraph?

A: No, Sir, I didn't.

Q: You came in the first time, and you told Ms. . . . do you remember talking to Ms. Ridenour the first time?

A: Yes, Sir.

Q: After, did you tell her you would show back up at her office?

A: Yes, Sir.

Q: Did you lie to her about that?

A: Yes, Sir, I did.

Q: Did you . . . did the FBI have to come to chase you around to get you?

A: Sir, the reason I didn't return was because, as you know, Mr. Williams is my friend, and I didn't want to say anything to have him sitting over there or nothing like that. So, yes, I did run because I didn't want to get up here.

Q: On the first occasion you had to meet Ms. Ridenour, did you tell her basically what you told us here today?

A: I didn't tell her anything, Sir. I told her that my statement was my first statement to her—they asked me did I receive any money from Mr. Williams, and my statement was, "No, Sir—I received it right outside my apartment."

Q: You told Ms. Ridenour you received marijuana from

Mr. Williams, didn't you?

A: I told her I received some marijuana outside of an apartment building when I came back. Then she told me to comeback Saturday and talk to her, so we can see exactly what's going on. But, you know, when it was time for me to come back Saturday and see her, I didn't come back.

Q: You called and lied to her again, didn't you?

A: The reason why I called was--

Q: You lied to her when you called her again, didn't you?

A: Mr. Clark, Yes. I told her I would come and meet her, and I did not come to meet her.

THE COURT: Mr. Clark, you are being repetitious.

MR. CLARK:

Q: You were using drugs, were you not?

A: Yes, Sir.

Q: You had a long history with cocaine, didn't you?

A: Yes, Sir.

Q: You were using cocaine at that time, weren't you?

A: Yes, Sir.

Q: Agent Ducote came out to meet you in a hotel down in Tillman's Corner, did he not?

A: Yes, Sir.

Q: And, Agent Ducote came out there and asked you who you were, didn't he? Do you remember the FBI agent who arrested you?

A: Yes, Sir.

Q: Did you lie to him?

A: About what?

Q: About who you were?

A: No, Sir.

Q: You were trying to run from the FBI, weren't you?

A: Yes, Sir.

Q: Alright. And, you have been detained in jail ever since, haven't you?

A: Yes, Sir.

Q: Look at your plea agreement. Among other things, is that the government can—look at page three, please, Sir. And, if I fail to testify, the government can tear up your plea agreement, can't they?

A: Yes, Sir.

MR. CLARK: That's all we have. Judge.

REDIRECT EXAMINATION

MS. GRIFFIN:

Q: Mr. Ward?

A: Yes, Ma'am.

Q: When we interviewed you, what did we tell you?

A: To tell the truth.

Q: Were you told what to say?

A: No, Ma'am, I was not.

Q: Okay—what, specifically, were you told to do in the courtroom?

A: You told me to tell the truth.

Q: Now, Mr. Ward, you plead guilty. Is your plea agreement up there?

A: Yes, Ma'am.

Q: To one count that subjects you to a sentence of up to twenty years?

A: Yes, Ma'am.

Q: And, to one count that carries a sentence of ten years—is that right?

A: Yes, Ma'am.

Q: The amount you plead guilty to subjects you to zero to twenty—the amount of marijuana, is that right?

A: Yes, Ma'am.

Q: So, there is no statutory enhancement, a required twenty. The zero to twenty doesn't become ten, fifteen, twenty. Do you understand that? That it's only a sentence of five to forty that becomes ten to life . . .

MR. CLARK: Judge, I'm sorry—I object to her leading the witness. He's testified what he thought the deal was.

THE COURT: Well, I think Mr. Clark is probably right, Ms. Griffin. Restate your question.

MS. GRIFFIN:

Q: You're facing up to twenty years—is that correct?

A: Yes, Ma'am.

Q: You're facing up to ten years on the counterfeiting charge?

A: Yes, Ma'am.

Q: What you actually receive on that is based on your guidelines, is that right?

A: Yes, Ma'am.

Q: Tell us what you understand your guidelines to be.

A: With the level I'm in, eighteen to twenty-four months. But, the judge do not have to go for it. It says in my plea agreement—it says it right here on the plea agreement.

Q: What page?

A: Page two. "That defendant to a sentence to above will subject the defendant to a sentence of twenty years and a maximum fine of one million and both, and a term of supervised release for at least three years. A mandatory special assessment fee of a hundred dollars as to Count One. And, a sentence of ten years, a maximum fine of two hundred and fifty on both of—on both. And, a term of supervised release of at least three years, and a mandatory special assessment fee of one hundred dollars as to Count Five."

Q: You were facing a mandatory twenty, weren't you, Sir?

MR. CLARK: Judge, I object to that. That's not the law.

MS. GRIFFIN: Judge, it is. I would like to approach . . .

THE COURT: Wait. Whether it's the law or not, it's the

witness's perception of what he thought he was facing at the time he entered into the plea agreement. So you know, you are in effect, I think, Ms. Griffin . . .

MS. GRIFFIN: Could we approach, Your Honor?

THE COURT: Let's finish up with whatever else we have and, if we need to hear it up here, we will.

MS. GRIFFIN:

Q: Mr. Ward, when you went to Dallas and first met— and, were paid by the individual nine hundred dollars for Sherman Williams—did something happen while you were out there about Mr. Williams's career?

A: Yes, Ma'am.

Q: What was that?

A: Mr. Williams had got cut off the football team.

Q: When was that?

A: That was the time I was up there, and purchased marijuana. That's when I went and paid the guy.

Q: When was that?

A: That was in . . . that was in '99. It had to be '98 or '99. I really don't know which year, but it was after I had got out of jail, though.

Q: After he got cut from the Dallas Cowboys while you were out there, he did not play professional football again, did he?

A: He had got cut. They called him back for one year—I think a guy got hurt. A guy got hurt, or something . . .

Q: After the fall of '99, he did not play professional football?

MR. CLARK: Judge, I object. That's misleading . . .

THE COURT: You can ask—I guess that was in the form of a question. That was a form of a question.

MR. CLARK: It's a misleading question, Judge.

THE COURT: Well, it was a question. It was a question. Did he play after the fall of '99 is what she asked. Ms. Griffin asked it that way.

MS. GRIFFIN:

Q: Do you know whether Sherman Williams played professional football after the fall of 1999?

A: No, Ma'am.

Q: Had he been cut at that time?

A: Yes, Ma'am.

Q: So, he was unemployed as a football player after the fall of '99?

A: Yes, Ma'am.

MS. GRIFFIN: That's all we have.

THE COURT: Okay. Ladies and Gentlemen—let's take our fifteen minute break. We'll call you back up at about three o'clock.

(RECESS)

THE COURT: Alright. Ms. Griffin, your next witness.

MS. GRIFFIN: We call Demetric Beans.

DEMETRIC BEANS

The witness, after first been duly sworn to tell the truth, the whole truth, and nothing but the truth, was examined and testified as follows:

MS. GRIFFIN:

Q: Tell us your name please, Ma'am.

A: My name is Demetric Beans.

Q: Can you spell your first name?

A: D-E-M-E-T-R-I-C.

Q: Ms. Beans, where do you live—in what city?

A: I live in Dallas, Texas.

Q: How are you employed?

A: I'm an exotic entertainer.

Q: Ms. Beans, did you enter a guilty plea to aiding and abetting Sherman Williams in an interstate travel case?

A: Yes.

Q: Is that in connection with marijuana?

A: Yes, Ma'am.

Q: As part of your plea agreement, did you agree to provide substantial assistance to the United States?

A: Yes, Ma'am.

Q: And, do you hope to receive a lighter sentence because of that?

A: I hope so.

Q: Who determines the sentence you will receive?

A: I guess the government.

Q: Do you know that it's the court that sentences you?

A: Uh-huh.

Q: Ms. Beans, when you lived in Dallas, Texas, in '97 through the spring of 2000, did you have a telephone number?

A: Yes, I did.

Q: What area code was that?

A: 9-7-2.

Q: What were your numbers?

A: 235-5797.

Q: Did that number change?

A: Well, that's my new number now.

Q: What was your old number?

A: I think it was 214-553 . . . I can't remember that number. It's an old number.

Q: Did you have a number 235-9606

A: Yes, I did.

Q: That was area code 9-7-2?

A: Uh-huh.

Q: In whose names were those phone numbers—those with 2-3-5 numbers?

A: In my son's name.

Q: What is that?

A: Demetrius Sanders.

Q: Now, that is a young person, is that correct?

A: Yeah. my son is twelve.

Q: And, he lives with you in Dallas?

A: He lives with my mother.

Q: Did you meet a Demetrius Sanders through Sherman Williams?

A: Yes, I did.

MR. CLARK: Judge, I object to her constant leading. I know this is peripheral, but would you ask her to ask . . .

THE COURT: I don't think that is particularly leading. Overruled.

MS. GRIFFIN:

Q: Is the Demetrius Sanders you met with Sherman Williams different from your son, Demetrius Sanders?

A: Yes.

Q: Ms. Beans, how did you meet Sherman Williams?

A: I met him at a nightclub.

Q: Approximately when was that?

A: In '96.

Q: What city?

A: In Dallas.

Q: And, you have known Sherman Williams since '96?

A: Yes, Ma'am.

Q: What was the nature of your relationship with Sherman Williams?

A: He was my boyfriend.

Q: Do you see him in the courtroom today?

A: Yes.

Q: Can you point him out? Can you tell me what he is wearing?

A: A gray suit.

Q: During the course of your relationship, did Sherman Williams ever come to your apartment?

A: Yeah—plenty of times.

Q: Where was that apartment located?

A: In Dallas.

Q: Okay. Did there ever come a time when you learned something about drugs and Sherman Williams?

A: Yes.

Q: Could you tell us approximately when that was?

A: Probably about the end of '98.

Q: What happened? What did he ask you?

A: Did I have any kind of connection, or something.

Q: Did he tell you what he meant by connections?

A: Did I know where to find marijuana from . . .

Q: What did you tell him?

A: I told him yeah.

Q: How is it you knew some individuals you could get marijuana from?

A: I know a whole bunch of people.

Q: Through your employment?

A: Well, yeah. That, too . . .

Q: So, did you assist him?

A: Yes, I did.

Q: How did you assist him?

A: I went out to meet new people, so we can get some deals going on.

Q: What do you mean by 'get some deals going on?'

A: So we can get some marijuana.

Q: Where did you meet these individuals—you and Sherman Williams?

A: In my house.

Q: How is it they would be at your house?

A: Like, what?

Q: Pardon?

A: Like, what you mean?

Q: Would you invite them to your house?

A: Yeah. I call them from my house, and they come over.

Q: What would happen when they came over?

A: They have marijuana. We give them money.

Q: Who would give them money?

A: Mr. Williams.

Q: Ms. Beans, do you know Frank Freeman?

A: Yes, I do.

Q: How did you meet Frank Freeman?

A: Through Mr. Williams.

Q: When did you meet Frank Freeman?

A: Probably, like, '96 also.

Q: I want to direct your attention to April 20th of 2000. Did you see Frank Freeman on that day?

A: April 20th? If I'm not mistaken, yeah. I think he was there.

Q: Was he at your apartment?

A: Yeah.

Q: Did he have another man with him?

A: I think it was him, Shack, and Demetrius Sanders.

Q: Alright. I am talking about addressing your attention to the time of Sherman's arrest—the day or two before Sherman's arrest. Was Frank Freeman at your apartment?

A: By himself?

Q: By himself . . .

A: No.

Q: Sherman Williams?

A: Well, yeah. Him and Sherman Williams was there by they-self.

Q: What happened when Sherman Williams, Frank Freeman, and you were at your apartment on or about April 20th?

A: We got some marijuana that day.

Q: Who is 'we?'

A: Me and Mr. Williams.

Q: Who did you purchase it from?

A: I can't recall who it was.

Q: Did someone come there to your apartment to deliver the marijuana?

A: Yes.

Q: How was the marijuana packaged?

A: In a trash bag.

Q: Who paid for the marijuana?

A: Mr. Williams.

Q: Do you know how much marijuana it was?

A: Well, when he would buy the stuff, he would get anywhere from fifty to a hundred pounds.

Q: Did you see the marijuana when Frank Freeman was there?

A: Yes.

Q: How was it packaged?

A: It probably was in individual big baggies. Something like that. But, in a big trash bag.

Q: Like a Glad bag, or some type of bag you would use in a kitchen?

A: Yeah.

Q: Okay—did Frank Freeman leave with the marijuana Sherman Williams purchased?

A: Yes, he did.

Q: Do you know what Frank Freeman was driving the last time?

A: I think he was in the gold Jetta, if I'm not mistaken.

Q: Sometime after Frank Freeman left, did you learn he had been arrested while transporting the marijuana back to Mobile?

A: No—I didn't know that until later on.

Q: Ms. Beans, do you know Demetrius Thomas?

A: Yes, I do.

Q: How did you know Demetrius Thomas?

A: Through Mr. Williams.

Q: Did you know Demetrius Thomas by a street name?

A: Yeah.

Q: What was that?

A: Shack.

Q: Did Demetrius Thomas ever come to your apartment in Texas?

A: Yes, he did.

Q: Why did he come to your apartment?

A: To pick up marijuana.

Q: When Demetrius Thomas would be at your apartment to pick up marijuana, who would be there with him?

A: Sometime, Mr. Williams and, sometime, Demetrius Sanders.

Q: Who is Demetrius Sanders?

A: I think his nickname is Knee.

Q: How did you meet Demetrius Sanders?

A: Through Mr. Williams.

Q: On how many occasions did Shack or Demetrius Thomas come to your apartment?

A: Probably come up there probably two or three times out of a week.

Q: Two or three times?

A: Uh-huh. Out of a week . . .

Q: Alright. Were there occasions where Demetrius Sanders came to your apartment alone? I mean, without Demetrius Thomas?

A: No.

Q: Ms. Beans, each time Demetrius Thomas and Demetrius Sanders came to your apartment, why were they there?

A: To purchase marijuana.

Q: Would you call someone for them? Someone they could purchase marijuana from?

A: Yes, I would.

Q: How many other times when Demetrius Thomas and Demetrius Sanders came to your apartment to buy marijuana was Sherman Williams there?

A: He was there quite a few times.

Q: Who would pay for the marijuana when Sherman Williams, Demetrius Thomas, or Demetrius Sanders were there?

A: Mr. Williams.

Q: What would happen to the marijuana Mr. Williams purchased?

A: They bring it back to Alabama with them.

Q: How do you know that?

A: Well, they will put it in the car, and they leave before he leaves.

Q: Who would leave before who leaves?

A: Demetrius Thomas and Demetrius Sanders would leave before Mr. Williams leave.

Q: Why was that?

A: Because they were his runners.

Q: Who were they runners for?

A: Mr. Williams.

Q: Ms. Beans, I want to direct your attention to the first week of April 2000. Did you see Demetrius Thomas on an occasion just before he got arrested?

A: Yes, I did—he had just left my house.

Q: What did he have with him?

A: He had some marijuana with him.

Q: Where had he gotten that marijuana?

A: From my house.

Q: Who paid for that marijuana at your house?

A: Mr. Williams.

Q: Do you know the exact weight of that marijuana?

A: Not exactly.

Q: Now, Ms. Beans, did you later learn that Demetrius Thomas had been arrested?

A: Yes, I did.

Q: How did you learn that?

A: He was calling my house, collect.

Q: Did you learn his girlfriend who was with him was arrested also?

A: Yes, I did.

Q: Were you asked to assist in making bond for her?

A: Yes, I was.

Q: Who asked you to assist her?

A: Mr. Williams.

Q: What did you do to assist Demetrius Thomas's girlfriend in making bond?

A: Me and Mr. Williams drove to Alabama, and I met her grandmother and aunt.

Q: Whose grandmother and aunt?

A: Shemara.

Q: Demetrius Thomas's girlfriend?

A: Uh-huh.

Q: Ms. Beans, where did you get the money to assist Demetrius Thomas's girlfriend?

A: Mr. Williams.

Q: What did you do with the money?

A: I gave it to her grandmother.

Q: Where did that take place? What city?

A: It took place here in Alabama—in Mobile.

Q: Ms. Beans, do you know Roderick Ward?

A: Yes, I do.

Q: How do you know Roderick Ward?

A: Through Mr. Williams.

Q: Do you know Roderick Ward by another name?

A: Juice.

Q: How long have you been knowin' Roderick Ward?

A: I have been knowing him about four or five years.

Q: Did Roderick Ward ever come to your apartment in Texas?

A: Yes, he did.

Q: Would he be with Sherman Williams?

A: Sometimes.

Q: What was the purpose of Roderick Ward's being at your apartment?

A: To purchase marijuana.

Q: Was Sherman Williams present when Roderick Ward purchased marijuana at your apartment?

A: Sometimes.

Q: Okay. Now, were you selling the marijuana to Roderick Ward?

A: What do you mean, 'was I selling?'

Q: Were you the one providing it to Roderick Ward?

A: Yes.

Q: Did some man come there to actually deliver the marijuana?

A: Yes.

Q: How did that man come to your apartment to deliver marijuana to Roderick Ward?

A: I just called him up and tell him what I need, and they come over.

Q: Who would Roderick Ward purchase the marijuana from?

A: Mr. Williams.

Q: When Mr. Williams was present, Roderick Ward was present, and marijuana was being purchased, who would be paying for the marijuana?

A: Mr. Williams.

Q: Ms. Beans, did there come a time when you received money by Money Gram?

A: Yes.

Q: Who sent you the money?

A: Juice did. I think it was about eighty dollars.

Q: Why were you expecting money from Juice?

A: Well, he wired it for Mr. Williams. I guess he didn't want to send it hisself—I don't know.

Q: Why were you receiving money from Mr. Williams?

A: Well, at the time, he was trying to pay for me to go to driving school.

Q: Did there come a time when Sherman Williams came by himself to pick up marijuana?

A: Well, if he come, he didn't really come by himself because he didn't want to drive it back by himself.

Q: Did he tell you that?

A: Well, I know that for a fact.

Q: Ms. Beans, did you make the profit off the marijuana that was sold at your apartment?

A: No.

Q: Who was making the—who was receiving the money that was being paid for the marijuana?

A: Mr. Williams was.

Q: He received the money when it was sold?

A: I guess so. I wasn't making no money off of it.

Q: You didn't receive any of the proceeds, right?

A: No.

Q: Ms. Beans, have you tested positive for the use of cocaine since you were released on bond?

A: That's what they say.

Q: That is in connection with some activities of your employment?

A: I don't do cocaine, though . . .

Q: You were with someone who does, is that right?

A: Yes. That's correct.

Q: You understand a revocation has been filed on your behalf?

A: Yes, I do.

Q: And, that we are seeking to have your bond revoked?

A: Yeah.

MS. GRIFFIN: That's all we have of this witness, Your Honor.

CROSS EXAMINATION

MR. CLARK:

Q: Ms. Beans, my name is Bob Clark. I don't believe we have ever met before, have we?

A: No, we haven't.

Q: I would like to ask you a few questions please, Ma'am. The plea agreement, Ms. Beans—do you recall signing a plea agreement with the United States attorney here in Mobile?

A: Yes.

Q: Okay. Now, you were indicted at some point in time, were you not?

A: I was subpoenaed.

Q: Were you indicted? You were charged with marijuana possession with intent to distribute, a conspiracy, weren't you?

A: Yes.

Q: You went to a probation conference where they told you your sentence could range anywhere from five years to twenty years, didn't they?

A: No. Anywhere from three to five years.

Q: That's what you plead guilty to—you plead guilty to interstate transportation. But, originally, you were charged with conspiracy to distribute, weren't you?

A: No—not that I'm aware of.

Q: Okay. Now, did the government tell you they were going to make a recommendation when you were indicted?

A: A recommendation like what?

Q: On your plea agreement there, please, Ma'am. Did they tell you that? Did they say they would recommend— they would tell the Judge, and ask for a downward departure?

A: They probably did.

Q: You had an attorney named Art Powell?

A: Yeah.

Q: That plea agreement there before you—now, look at it to see if that bears your signature, and your attorneys signature.

A: My signature is not on there.

Q: I'm sorry—your signature is not on there?

A: No.

THE COURT: The original may be in the court file. Why don't you ask her if she signed one . . .

MR. CLARK:

Q: Let me show you this plea agreement that has your name on it, and ask you if you signed one just like this one.

A: Yes, I did.

Q: And, you understand the government was going to give you some consideration for your testimony?

A: Yeah.

Q: But, you had to provide substantial assistance, didn't you?

A: Yes.

Q: Substantial assistance means more than just assisting the government. You had to provide a body count—the more you told, the better deal you were going to cut, wasn't it?

A: Well, I wouldn't say that.

Q: Well, what do you expect your eventual sentence to be, Ms. Beans?

A: I'm not for sure yet.

Q: You were supposed to get probation?

A: Supposed to . . .

Q: Yes, Ma'am, I understand that. At the time that y'all negotiated your plea to this interstate transportation, it was your understanding—or, your hope—to get probation, is that right?

A: At that time, yeah. But, it's probably going to change now.

Q: Right, because the government says you have been doing cocaine?

A: I don't do cocaine.

Q: I didn't say you did, Ma'am. I'm saying the government said you did.

A: Yeah.

Q: They said you are doing cocaine and, now, the deal is off, right?

A: Probably so.

Q: In the plea agreement, you agreed to take a polygraph test in order to determine whether or not you were lying to the government, didn't you?

A: Yes.

Q: Did you ever take a polygraph test?

A: No, but I am willing to take one.

Q: Okay. You met Mr. Williams in 1996, did you not?

A: Yes, I did.

Q: But, you never did any kind of supplying to anybody until 1999, did you?

A: '98.

Q: '98. What month?

A: What month?

Q: Yes, Ma'am. Do you recall?

A: No, I don't.

Q: Do you recall testifying before the grand jury here in Mobile?

A: Yes, I do.

Q: And, that was back on June of 2000, right?

A: Yes.

Q: At that time, did you tell the grand jury this has been only going on for one year?

A: I have—about a year, or year and a half.

Q: No, Ma'am. Didn't you say one year?

A: A year—year and a half, or something like that.

Q: Let me show you—first of all, this is a transcript. You went before the grand jury back on the 28th of June of this year, is that correct?

A: Yes.

Q: And, that was after you made you deal with the government?

A: Yes, you can say that.

Q: Okay. Do you recall being asked about the marijuana business?

A: Uh-huh.

Q: And, a juror asked you, "The marijuana business just started up last year, no other time in the past?" What was your answer to that?

A: No.

Q: You didn't say a year and a half—when he said it was last year, you said there was nothing in the past. You said no, right?

A: Yeah—there was nothing in the past.

Q: Okay—past a year. Now, with regard to the marijuana business, you had all the contacts out in Dallas, didn't you?

A: I wouldn't say that—but, I know people.

Q: Well, then, the people you called were the people you knew, weren't they?

A: No—it was people that I met.

Q: At the club?

A: Or, wherever.

Q: Well, you had the contacts for marijuana, didn't you?

A: No, sometimes Mr. Williams would tell me to meet people.

Q: Let me show you a transcript again, please, Ma'am. Page six. You were asked by Ms. Dow, "How did you know the number to call for these individuals?" Tell the ladies and gentlemen of the jury your answer.

A: On the transcript it says I knew them myself.

Q: Read the whole answer.

A: "And, so, I went out to meet different people to try certain stuff."

Q: So, you are the one who had the contacts for all the marijuana, weren't you?

A: Well, some of the people I did know.

Q: Some of the people you knew?

A: Yeah. But, I didn't do business with people that I

knew. These are people that I met in the club.

Q: People you met at the club. People you met. People you knew?

A: Yeah.

Q: That's how it got set up, wasn't it?

A: Not really.

Q: Okay. Now, you recall Ms. Dow asking you at the grand jury, "Tell me who those people were." She asked you about their numbers, is that correct? Their telephone numbers? How to get in touch with these people?

A: Yeah.

Q: You told her all of them changed their numbers, and moved and stuff . . .

A: Well, they all did change their numbers once all of this started going on.

Q: You didn't tell her anything about any of your suppliers out in Dallas, did you?

A: I don't know none of their numbers no more.

Q: I didn't ask you about the numbers.

A: No, I didn't.

Q: Now, Shack is the one that came and did business with you, is he not?

A: Yeah, at times.

Q: Well, let's look at page eight of your transcript. Says here, "What was the general procedure with the marijuana? Was it at your house to be picked up? Explain to the Grand

Jury, generally, what would happen." What did you say?

A: They come picked it up.

Q: What would happen like that? Like, what? You asked Ms. Dow, what would happen. "Like what," right?

A: Yeah.

Q: Ms. Dow's other question was, "How would it come to be picked up?" What did you tell Ms. Dow at that time?

A: Shack.

Q: Read the transcript—what you said at that time.

A: Well, Shack had come to pick it up, and he had the money. He was the one with money.

Q: Okay.

A: Shack.

Q: That's what you told Ms. Dow back on June 28th of this year, isn't it?

A: Yeah.

Q: You told her—she asked you how all of this worked, didn't she?

A: Yes, she did.

Q: And, you explained to her how it worked—that Shack came and got it, and Shack brought the money, didn't you?

A: Yeah.

Q: You knew Shack then didn't you?

A: Through Mr. Williams, yeah.

Q: You knew Shack. Did you know Frank Freeman?

A: Yes.

Q: You knew Frank Freeman well, didn't you?

A: How well are you talking about?

Q: Well, did you have a nickname for Mr. Freeman?

A: Yes.

Q: What was that nickname?

A: Pervert.

Q: Did that relate to something?

THE COURT: Well, it doesn't matter. That's consistent with what we heard him saying—it doesn't matter.

MR. CLARK: Okay—I'll move on. I don't want to embarrass myself.

THE COURT: Okay.

MR. CLARK:

Q: You knew Mr. Freeman pretty well, right?

A: I wouldn't say that. But, I knew him . . .

Q: You knew Mr. Ward?

A: Yeah, I know Mr. Ward.

Q: You knew Mr. Thomas?

A: Yeah.

Q: You knew Mr. Sanders?

A: Yeah.

Q: They are the ones who came and picked up the marijuana from you?

A: Exactly—yeah.

Q: Now, on April the 21st of this year, do you recall Mr. Freeman's being at your house?

A: Yeah—Frank? Yeah . . .

Q: And, you said . . . I believe you testified he was in a Jetta, and that someone came and brought the marijuana?

A: Uh-huh.

Q: Is that correct?

A: Yes.

Q: Brought it to your apartment?

A: Yes.

Q: And, you saw it with your own eyes?

A: Yeah.

Q: There is no question that it came to your apartment?

A: Yeah, it came to my apartment.

Q: Who took it out, and put it in the trunk of the Jetta?

A: It depends. Probably both of them—Mr. Williams or Mr. Freeman at the time.

Q: Okay. Let's talk about April 21st, okay?

A: Okay.

Q: Who took the packages down?

A: I can't really recall, but, it was either one of them, if not both of them.

Q: Okay. Now, did you ever receive any money for what you were doing?

A: No, I didn't.

Q: Mr. Williams never laid any bills for you or anything?

A: No, he didn't.

Q: You had never been to his home in Dallas, had you?

A: No, I went to one of . . . some apartments that he had, or something.

Q: Here is the question I want to ask you. On page twenty-four of your transcript, one of the jurors asked you, "You didn't know them prior to Sherman Williams telling you who they were?" What was your answer? If you would read the entire answer to the jury . . .

A: I have on here I knew them—I was the one that introduced them to him. So, I did know them . . .

Q: So, before the grand jury, you were sworn to tell the truth, weren't you?

A: Yes, I was.

Q: And, you told the grand jury at that time that you were the one who introduced them to Sherman Williams?

A: Introduced who to Sherman Williams?

Q: In your grand jury testimony, you said it usually worked that Shack came out, brought the money, picked it up, and brought it back. You knew the suppliers of the marijuana?

A: Yeah.

Q: You never received any money for it?

A: No, I didn't.

MR. CLARK: That's all we have, Judge.

REDIRECT EXAMINATION

MS. GRIFFIN:

Q: Ms. Beans, you testified before the grand jury in June of 2000?

A: Yes, Ma'am.

Q: You told them this had been going on at your residence about a year, is that right?

A: Yes, Ma'am.

Q: Do you have a grand jury testimony there in front of you?

A: Uh-huh.

Q: Would you turn to page five?

A: Okay.

Q: Were you asked what your involvement was at the top of the page, line 3, on page five?

A: Okay.

Q: Read line three—were you asked what was your involvement?

A: Uh-huh.

Q: What did you tell Ms. Dow?

A: I just called the people.

Q: Would you look at line nineteen on page five?

A: Okay.

Q: Were you asked why you were calling these people?

A: Yes.

Q: What did you tell the grand jury?

A: Because he told me to call them.

Q: Who was the 'he' you were referring to?

A: Mr. Williams.

Q: Look on page six, lines three through ten. Were you asked the names of the people who brought the marijuana?

A: Yes, I did.

Q: Did you give those names?

A: Yes.

Q: Would you look at page seven, line three? Were you asked how many times did you set up marijuana connections between Bear, LT, D, and Sherman Williams?

A: I said six or seven times, or more.

Q: Would you turn to page nine, line two? Were you asked who arranged for Demetrius Thomas, Frank, Juice, and Demetrius Sanders to come and pick up the marijuana?

A: I said Sherman.

MS. GRIFFIN: That's all we have, Your Honor.

THE COURT: Your next witness . . .

MS. GRIFFIN: Call Dana Ridenour.

THE COURT: Agent Ridenour?

DANA RIDENOUR

MS. GRIFFIN:

Q: Tell us your name.

A: Dana Ridenour.

Q: How are you employed?

A: I'm a special agent with the Federal Bureau of Investigation.

Q: How many years of law enforcement experience do you have?

A: Five.

Q: Ms. Ridenour, I want to direct your attention to April 21st of 2000. Were you concealed in Frank Freeman's apartment?

A: Yes, Ma'am.

Q: Where were you hiding?

A: I was hiding in a bedroom adjacent to the living room

area.

Q: Could you hear what was going on in the other room?

A: Yes, Ma'am. We had cameras set up, so I could see, as well.

Q: Now, thereafter, the next day or two, did you receive the black bag Sherman Williams carried into that apartment?

A: Yes, Ma'am.

Q: Did you search this bag?

A: Yes, Ma'am.

Q: Did you find a cellular telephone in the bag?

A: Yes, Ma'am, we did.

Q: What brand telephone was in the bag?

A: It's a Nokia phone made by Bell South.

Q: Were you able to turn that phone on?

A: Yes, Ma'am.

Q: What's the number for that telephone in the black bag?

A: Well, when I turned it on, the name Shake 20 pops up. And, the telephone number is 334-591-3233.

Q: Were you able to determine some of the numbers last called by that cellular phone?

A: Yes, Ma'am. We scrolled through the numbers. He has a directory on there of numbers he keeps.

Q: Is there a number for Rice on there?

A: If you go down to the Rs, there is K. Rice, 256-565-3815, dash H, which would be 256-355-6369.

Q: Ms. Ridenour, based on that, did you subpoena a number of telephone records?

A: Yes, Ma'am, I did.

Q: Did you receive those telephone tolls?

A: Yes, Ma'am, we did.

Q: In whose name is that phone?

A: It's in Sherman Williams's name.

Q: In Dallas, Texas?

A: Yes.

Q: Did you receive Demetric Beans's tolls?

A: Yes, Ma'am, we did.

Q: In whose name are those?

A: There were two numbers for Demetric Bean, and they were both under the name of Demetrius Sanders.

MS. GRIFFIN: That's all I have of this witness at this time, Your Honor.

THE COURT: Alright.

CROSS EXAMINATION

MR. CLARK: No cross, Judge.

THE COURT: Okay, you can step down.

MS. GRIFFIN: At this time the United States will rest.

THE COURT: Alright. Ladies and Gentlemen, you just heard Ms. Griffin say the United States rests. That means the government has concluded the presentation of their evidence in their case in chief.

(Jury not Present)

THE COURT: Counsel, can I see you at sidebar just a minute?

(At sidebar)

THE COURT: Alright. Arthur.

MR. MADDEN: Your Honor, on behalf of Mr. Williams, we move for a judgment of acquittal with respect to each, or the counts of the superseding indictment. We argue the government has failed to make a prima facie case which rose to each of the elements in each of those counts.

THE COURT: Okay. Having heard the evidence, I am convinced the evidence is sufficient as construed in the light most favorable to the government upon which the jury could find beyond a reasonable doubt the defendant was guilty of the crime. So, the motion is denied.

Alright. Let's go off the record a minute and visit . . .

(An off-the-record discussion was held. Then, a recess.)

THOUGHTS

DECEMBER 6, 2000

By the morning of December 6, 2000, the last day of the trial, I'm not sure how I managed it, but I overcame the skepticism about whether or not the trial was going to take place since we completed the second day. I reconciled it would happen, but I still wasn't sure about the verdict—all I could do was hope for a 'not guilty' . . .

As with the first two days of my trial, friends and family were with me—it warmed my heart they stuck it out. But, I couldn't help feeling disappointment in those I thought were my friends. It was a bitter pill to learn they deserted me when I needed them most, but I guess I shouldn't have been surprised. It was during those difficult three days I learned friendship—to some—is cheap, and loyalty is non-existent. Didn't they realize the result would be losing the very career that afforded me the opportunity to assist them financially and give them opportunities to grow as people? If they did, it made little difference in their decision to throw me under the bus to save themselves from a lengthy prison sentence. Their actions hurt my heart—I value friendship, and it seemed as though they had no concept of what it means to be a friend.

Then, there was my attorney—he wasn't giving me any indication of my walking away as a free man. I always asked, "What do you think our chances are for getting a not guilty verdict? How do you think the trial is going?"

No response.

As I woke up on the morning of the last day of the trial—the third day—I felt different. I still wasn't sure if the verdict were going to be guilty or not guilty, and the uncertainty left me with knots in my stomach. My mother, though, still stood by my side, confident I could handle whatever God had planned for me. She never lost her faith—not for a second.

Then, it was time. No one spoke as guards accompanied me to the courtroom. Over the previous days, I came to the conclusion my attorney wasn't the right guy for the job—I didn't think he cared if I would be free or locked up. I got the distinct impression he was going through the motions because he felt I was going to be found guilty.

I felt different when I took my seat at the defendant's table.

I didn't know what to think.

THE THIRD DAY

DECEMBER 6, 2000

UNITED STATES OF AMERICA (plaintiff) vs.
SHERMAN WILLIAMS (defendant)

THE COURT: Good morning, Ladies and Gentlemen. Glad to have you back this morning. Alright—the defense can proceed now, Mr. Clark.

MR. CLARK: Yes, Sir, Judge. Judge, Ms. Griffin and I agreed if I call certain witnesses—some of the witnesses are from out of state—and, in order to allow us to proceed, we agreed to certain stipulations.

THE COURT: Alright. Now, a stipulation, Ladies and Gentlemen, is an agreement the parties reached that if a witness were here, they would testify to the following facts. And, you may accept these facts and give them such weight you determine they are entitled to.

Alright. Mr. Clark.

MR. CLARK: Judge, the first witness we call is Bruce Ungstead with Remax in Texas. He provided us with documents that say since August of 1998, he was the property manager for Sherman Williams for his residence at 631 Allen in Coppel, Texas. The property was leased to the first tenant from August the 2nd of 1998, to the end of February of 1999, when she moved out. The property was then leased again beginning March the 3rd of 1999, until the end of October 2000, when the property was sold. We would offer that, Your Honor.

THE COURT: Alright.

MR. CLARK: The second document is a document as a result of a subpoena to the Dallas Cowboys with regard to Sherman Williams's pay. The document provides to us if the custodian of the records were to testify, he would testify as follows:

His gross pay for the following years: 1995, eight hundred and fifty-seven thousand, nine hundred and eighty-five dollars, and seventy-one cents. 1996, four hundred and twelve dollars . . . well, four hundred and twelve thousand dollars, seven hundred . . . four hundred twelve thousand, seven hundred forty-one dollars, and thirty-nine cents. 1997, four hundred seventeen thousand, six hundred and sixty-five dollars, and seventy-two cents. 1998, three hundred and three thousand, one hundred and eighteen dollars, and seventy-two cents. 1999, eighty-one thousand one hundred and seventy-six dollars and forty-seven cents. The total is two million, seventy-two thousand, six hundred and eighty-eight dollars, and a penny. We further agree if the custodian for the records for Duval Motors were called to testify, he would testify the 1992 Grand . . . Mercury Grand Marquis was purchased on November the 19th of 1999. Judge, we would further . . . if the custodian of records were called, even though it doesn't show in the document, he would testify Sherman Williams paid for the car on November the 19th, 1999. The last document is the violation of probation—violation of release on Frankie Freeman, showing he tested positive for cocaine on two occasions rather than one time. Those are our witnesses—if they were called, that's why they would testify to, Judge. Having introduced those, we rest.

THE COURT: Alright. The defendant has announced he rests his case. If the government has any rebuttal, they can call witnesses at this time. Ms. Griffin?

MS. GRIFFIN: Not at this time, Your Honor.

THE COURT: So, there is no rebuttal. You have heard all the evidence and all the testimony you're going to hear in the case. The things remaining to be done now before you begin your deliberations are closing arguments, then my instructions to you on the rules of the law.

ATTORNEYS' CLOSING ARGUMENTS

MS. GRIFFIN: Ladies and Gentlemen, I appreciate the attention you have paid to this case—it's obvious each of you have paid attention to it, and we appreciate that. You have now seen both sides of the hand, and you know from either direction it's a hand—just like you know this evidence shows you Sherman Williams is guilty as charged. Either side, he is guilty.

I told you in my opening this case is about greed, and you now have before you the financial documents. They show in 1998, he made five hundred and fifty-four thousand dollars less than he started out making. It shows you in 1999 he made seven hundred thousand, seventy-six hundred and nine dollars less legitimately than he had been making. He was virtually unemployed, and he didn't have the lifestyle of making eight hundred thousand dollars a year.

He had to make money, so he sent his friends—his childhood friends Roderick Ward, Frank Freeman, and others—to transport marijuana for him. And, he was there—he touched it and directed it, just like you saw him touch every piece of it on that video to see if it all were there, and he was still going to make money. He sent them to get it. He had them transport it distances, so he wouldn't be caught. He made efforts for that because he didn't ride with it. And, not until Frank Freeman taped him on the video could you see the entire workings of Sherman Williams's drug organization.

You will have the video. You may look at the video again—the court will tell you that. You can see all the evidence again. You know on the video you hear Sherman Williams say, "Is they individually packed, twenty-five each?" Talking about the money Frank Freeman owes him, Sherman says, "I don't never remember you making no trip, and didn't get nothing." That's because Frank Freeman, as you recall, made earlier trips. Williams says, "You owe me from the last two pounds I gave you . . ."

Two pounds of what? We're not talking about flour. We're not talking about candy. We're talking about drugs Sherman Williams can sell and keep that lifestyle because he's down seven hundred thousand dollars a year.

He goes on further to say, "You didn't see any police coming back," because he doesn't want to get caught—he can't keep taking this cash if people are caught. Now, remember—Sherman Williams doesn't know he's being recorded. And, Frank Freeman told you he wouldn't have made that trip where he got caught if Sherman Williams told him the truth. At the time on April the 29th that

Frank Freeman was transporting fifty pounds of marijuana for Sherman Williams, Demetrius Thomas—Shack—was sitting in a Texas jail having been caught April the 4th. Frank Freeman, remember, stopped transporting sometime in '99 for Sherman Williams because Sherman began to use Demetrius Thomas and Demetrius Sanders.

Sherman comes to Frank, and Frank asks, "Where's Shack?" Sherman says, "Now that Shack had been caught running marijuana," and Frank told you he wouldn't have gone if he had known that—so, Frank got caught, and he told them he was running for Sherman Williams.

You will also hear on the video they talk about the twelve hundred dollars—they talk about the money Kenneth Rice gave Sherman Williams in a hotel room in Jackson, Mississippi. You have the hotel records showing Kenneth Rice stayed at that Fairfield Inn in Jackson, Mississippi. He had the money that was obtained from the black bag, and that money went from Jackson, Mississippi, to Monroe, to Shreveport, to Tyler, and to Dallas—and, it came back with Sherman Williams and came from the black bag. Some twenty-four thousand dollars . . .

You will hear them talk on the tape, "Did you get the boys' yoda? Did you get his cocaine? Did you get Kenneth Rice's cocaine?" Sherman says, "No." Now, Sherman Williams? He's thinking about keeping that money. You hear Sherman Williams ask, "Y'all weigh all of those hoes up." And, they're not talking about women—they're talking about marijuana. Talking about marijuana, and they weighed them all.

You saw him pick each one up as though he were fascinated by it—that's what greed does to you. You see, he talked about real cases going in the back, and he's talking about the small bags he ultimately throws when the police come. The same small bags that had his fingerprints on them.

Most important, at the end of the tape, you have him tell Frank Freeman a story to say to the children you can hear at the end of the video outside of Frank's apartment. Sherman Williams said, "I'll just walk by the car, and then you say some shit like you still want me to take them clothes by your mama's house . . ." Well, these aren't clothes, and they're not going to anyone's mama's house!

The fifty pounds you see Sherman Williams take out like Santa Claus and throw it over his shoulder is what he does to make a living—and, he was caught this time. He's gotten by with it—he has gotten by with it as Roderick Ward ran for him, as Frank Freeman ran for him, and as Demetric Beans assisted him until he was videoed.

Now, what happens when he comes out of the house? He runs. You'll remember—you can hear at the end of the tape when you play it again—that they say, "Police! Mobile police! Get down! Get down!" And, you heard the officers tell you the place was lit up like Christmas with police cars. There is no mistaking they were officers, and they were there to arrest him. There is no mistaking when the letters are this big that say, 'Police,' and you are to stop. He ran because he wanted to continue his successful drug dealing.

Now, Ladies and Gentlemen, you will—for the first time—have with you the indictment. The four counts the court told you about. Count one is the conspiracy, and it covers the entire time, beginning to end. Count Two is the April the 4th, 2000 stop of Demetrius Thomas, and it charges an attempt.

Demetrius Thomas told you he left from Mobile, he met Sherman Williams in Texas, he picked up drugs in Texas, and he was transporting them back to deliver them in Mobile to Sherman Williams. He was attempting to bring that marijuana to Mobile with the assistance of Sherman

Williams, and for Sherman Williams. That comprises Count Two.

Count Three is the possession on March 2nd of 2000. Demetrius Thomas, the three pounds, and the Mercury— the Mercury Marquis in Saraland. You will remember that's where the gun was found, and you'll remember that's when Demetrius Thomas told the officers that . . .

Count Four involves another attempt on April the 20th. That's when Frank Freeman went from Mobile at Sherman Williams's request, picked up fifty pounds of marijuana, and was coming back to Mobile after Sherman paid for the marijuana in Texas. That's the attempt to come back with the fifty pounds with which Frank Freeman was arrested. That's the fifty pounds seen on the tape, and Sherman Williams is going through it, ultimately taking it with him out of the apartment, putting it in the Jetta.

Now—you'll remember as he got around the Jetta is when the officers told him to freeze, and he ran. He tossed two small bags of marijuana, and you can see him pinching off the top. Also, the next day, they found the key to the Jetta, right where Sherman Williams was stopped—right at the guide power pole was where the key was found. Where he tossed the key in his attempt to evade arrest and evade officers.

The court will charge you may consider flight as evidence of guilt. Obviously, if you're stopped by a policeman, are told to stop, and you have done nothing, you have no reason to fear. You have no reason to run. But, if you have done something and you want to flee to get away from the cops, you have to ask yourself why someone would run if they hadn't done anything?

Ladies and Gentlemen, regardless of what you do today, everyone on this list has plead to the felony convictions.

Roderick Ward is in jail. Demetrius Thomas is in jail. Demetrius Sanders is now deceased. Frank Freeman plead guilty, and is awaiting sentencing. The same for Demetric Beans—she plead guilty, and is awaiting sentencing. And, the reason for that is they were all in the game with Sherman Williams. They worked for him and were at his bidding—he, too, is guilty just as they have admitted their guilt.

We ask you, as I told you in the opening, to return a verdict that is just, fair, and speaks the truth. We contend Sherman Williams is guilty as charged in each and every count.

The court will tell you once you decide guilt or innocence, you have one more duty to do if you convict. We contend—and, the Court will tell you—you must find a special verdict as to quantity. The quantity of drugs involved in the case.

Now—you have before you a special verdict after you find he is guilty asking you if the conspiracy, Count One, the entire time involved more than one hundred kilograms of marijuana. You heard yesterday a kilogram is 2.2 pounds—so more than a hundred kilograms would be more than two hundred and twenty pounds. You will have that written and before you.

We submit to you Frank Freeman told you about three trips of twenty pounds, which makes sixty pounds. He told you about the fifty pounds that was seized, and he told you about a hundred-pound ripoff he was attempting to purchase with Demetrius Thomas and Demetric Beans.

Demetrius Thomas told you about the hundred pounds that were ripped—they went to purchase it and was ripped off. He told you he made trips of fifty pounds. Roderick Ward told you he made three trips of ten pounds, and he was present on the trip Demetrius Thomas told you about—a hundred pounds.

We don't double count the trips—that totals five hundred and forty pounds of marijuana. You have to find yes or no that the conspiracy involved more than two hundred and twenty. And, of course, it does. Ladies and Gentlemen, we ask you to listen carefully to Mr. Clark, and I submit to you he will not tell you it's not Sherman Williams on that video.

THE COURT: Alright. Mr. Clark . . .

MR. CLARK: May it please the court, ladies and gentlemen of the jury—good morning. This is my opportunity to tell you what I think the evidence has been in this case. First of all, I would like to thank you for your service—it's been a real pleasure to try this case in front of you.

The first thing I want to talk to you about is your job. You notice we all rise—everybody in the courtroom rises when you either come in or you leave, and the reason we do that is because you are judges. You didn't go to law school and you didn't go to school to be a judge, but, you are, in fact going to be judges this morning. When the judge gives you this case, you will judge this case based on the evidence you have heard in this courtroom.

Now, as you have seen during the trial of this case, if I make a mistake, Judge Butler can straighten me out. If Judge Butler makes a mistake, the Eleventh Circuit Court of Appeals can straighten it out. If you make a mistake, we will live with it for the rest of our lives. So, when you get in the jury room, you're going to see—you're going to feel the weight of this, and you're going to notice you have the most important job in this courtroom. The decision you make is the decision we all live with . . .

The judge will give you the law by which you will decide. He's going to tell you certain things, and one of the things is Sherman Williams comes into this courtroom presumed innocent.

That presumption, as I told you in the opening statement, follows him throughout the entire trial. It's like a cloak around his shoulder. He is presumed innocent. That's evidence on his behalf. And, that stays around him and attends him until and unless the government proves his guilt beyond a reasonable doubt.

Now, what's a reasonable doubt? The judge is going to tell you what a reasonable doubt is. We have all heard of it in our common, every day lives, and you're called to jury service because of your common sense. Your common sense tells you what having a reasonable doubt is—you've heard it throughout your life. Well, I'm going to give that person the benefit of the doubt—that's what it is. You're giving someone the benefit of the doubt.

Proof beyond a reasonable doubt is proof of such a convincing nature that you wouldn't hesitate to act on it in your every day ordinary business affairs. You have made decisions in your life prior to today that involve beyond a reasonable doubt. When you decided to get married, you thought to yourself, *I love this person, I want to marry this person, spend the rest of my life with this person*, and made the decision to get married. That was a decision you made beyond a reasonable doubt. Because, if we have doubt, we don't get married. The same thing when you bought a house. You decided on the house you wanted beyond a reasonable doubt.

Beyond a reasonable doubt is of such a convincing nature that, in an unprejudiced mind, it would bring an overriding belief in guilt. An overriding belief!

If you say, "Well, maybe he's guilty . . ." you know that's not sufficient. If you say, "Well, he's possibly guilty," it isn't sufficient, either. If you say, "Well, he's probably guilty," that's not sufficient—you have to say not guilty if it's maybe, possibly, or probably. You can only find him guilty if it is beyond a reasonable doubt. That's the standard in our society . . .

It's kind of like playing football—if you take the ball and run ninety-nine yards, you get no point. The only time you ever get the points is if you go past the hundred yard line. That hundred yard line is proof beyond a reasonable doubt— you can go to it, but you have to go beyond a reasonable doubt. And, the judge is going to tell you that's the standard. He's going to tell you what the law is.

When I first started practicing law, I would go home every night and, as a lawyer, you probably realize and understand the only people we ever consider is ourselves. I would go home at night, and it finally got to where nobody talked to me, but my wife. We'd sit down, have dinner, and talk. I would tell her what I did during my day, and how important it was to civilization.

Back in the early seventies, ladies used to knit afghans to put on the back of the couch, and my wife did, too. She was working on one night, and it was very intricate detail— she had to count so many stitches before she changed colors, or whatever. So, I was telling her about a case, and she was counting stitches. Finally, I said, "Well, what do you think?" She looked up at me, and she hadn't heard a word I said. She was counting, and she said, "Bob, what do you think is fair? That's basically why we're here . . ."

The government advised Sherman Williams of things. They have accused him. We have all been accused of things we didn't do, but we have been accused of it. That's why we're here today—he was accused. Simply accused by the government. Now, the government has to prove to twelve citizens beyond a reasonable doubt what they say is true. And, as the judge will tell you, there is no burden on Sherman to prove anything to you. It's not like in high school when a young man would go out with one of the cheerleaders—or, a beautiful young lady in high school—and he would come back Monday, and all the guys would say, "What was she like?" And, he would start talking about how great she was, and he would say things that maybe weren't true about her.

She could never prove it didn't happen—in fact, she may be stigmatized. You've known somebody who was stigmatized their entire high school career because they couldn't prove it didn't happen. That's why, in our society, the burden is on the government. If the government points a finger at you, comes in here, and says you did it, they have to prove it to twelve citizens in the community it happened.

Now, Ms. Griffin, in her opening statement, said this is about greed. "It's about greed. It's about money." Sherman Williams didn't have any money—he was unemployed. She's taken it down now, but you saw the contract, and the contract we introduced this morning will show you two million seventy-eight thousand dollars. And, Ms. Griffin says it's his lifestyle. His lifestyle? He bought a 1992 Mercury Marquis for his girlfriend. He was driving Toyota 4-Runner. Does this sound like some expense? Did she show you his big house here in Mobile and say, "Hey, look! This is what he bought . . ." No. Did she say, "Look at all the jewelry! Look at all the things he spent money on!" No. The truth is he's a very prudent individual. He had plenty of money, and he still has plenty of money.

But, the government wants you to say it's greed. Is that believable? Have they proven to you beyond a reasonable doubt? Have they? Have they shown he needed any money? Have they brought you the first bill, the first creditor, the first anything and said, "Look, this shows it!" Have they? I submit to you that they haven't.

Now, one of the things I ask you to look at is the factual

résumé I think sets the tone for this case—the résumé of Frank Freeman. It says in that factual résumé Sherman Williams was the target of that operation—the government targeted somebody. The government has a big bull's eye on Sherman Williams. That's who they want . . .

Now, what has the government done? What have they done to get the target of the operation? They have gone out and made deals with the devils themselves. Let me tell you something—the United States Code says if I find a witness, if I offer a witness and say, "Look, come in here—come in here and say this. I will give you a hundred bucks," it's like a little-bitty something. No big deal. I would go to the penitentiary for a long time. I really would.

But, yet, the government in this case has gone out and laid people something far more precious than silver and gold. They have gone out and bought testimony—bought this testimony with freedom. I don't know of any war this government has ever fought over money. I don't believe the Revolutionary War was fought over money. I don't believe the Civil War was fought over money. I don't believe World War I was fought over money. I don't believe World War II was fought over money. I think it was fought over freedom. Our freedom. My freedom. Your freedom. That's precious to us as American citizens—we want to live in a free society, and be free people.

That's why we organized this government. The government we're proud of because of what? Because of the freedom it offers us. Freedom! And, the government uses that as its currency to buy evidence—and, bring it before you.

Look at what these people expect by the way of the currency of freedom. You heard Demetric Beans say, "I expected probation. I don't use drugs." She told you she didn't use drugs, but they're going to revoke her plea agreement for using cocaine. Well, what did she expect? Probation. Who is the center of all this? Who set all of this up? Demetric Beans. But, they say, "Okay, you're not the target of the operation, so if you'll come in and say what we want you to say, we'll give you probation."

You heard Roderick Ward, and you heard what he said he expected to get. Twenty years. Look at his plea agreement and see if it doesn't say something about it. Listen to what he said—he said he expected to get eighteen to twenty-four months. Eighteen years of freedom. The government bought and paid for his testimony with eighteen years of freedom.

Frankie Freeman. Look at their plea agreements. Look at all the plea agreements. They have been bought and paid for—every single one of them—in the currency of freedom. Something for which our forefathers fathers fought hard. Do you think Washington, Jefferson, and Lincoln would be proud they fought for this freedom we enjoy if they knew the government was buying testimony? Do you think Madison, Marshall, and those people would be proud of our government if they knew they were spending the currency of freedom for testimony?

The judge will advise you can take into consideration what these people have been given—and, the fact they may want to do more to make a better deal with the government. They all want probation. They all want two years or less. Something minimum. And, now, I submit to you, they would do practically anything to get it.

If the termite man—the Terminex man—comes to the house and says, "Look, Mr. Clark, you've got termites. We can fix termites. We can take care of the termites. But, you're going to have to leave your house, as well as all your valuables in it, for about a half day while we poison the termites." If that termite inspector were Beans, Thomas, Freeman, or Ward, would you leave your valuables in your house? Would you leave valuables in the house for a half day while they came in and killed the termites? Well? Would you? Do you feel that comfortable with that?

Tell me which one of them you didn't think lied to you right here in front of you? How many of them do you think? I told you at the very beginning the government was going to bring out thieves, liars, and exotic dancers—and, that's what the government has provided you.

Let's go over some of their testimony—let's go over Mr. Freeman's testimony. On the stand, Mr. Freeman says he was a drug user, and you will have his drug test showing the probation department. I can't find it right now—I'm not going to waste time. Look at it—it says he turned up dirty urine. This is a guy the government called! They caught him in Saraland. They caught him in Texas. They let him out on the street. They gave him his freedom, so they could get the target. They let him out on the streets, and he used cocaine. Not marijuana—cocaine! They brought him back in and said, "Look, you have to stop this drug stuff." He said, "I promise to you I'll do it. I promise you, I'll obey the law. I told you—I will promise you—just let me go. I will obey the law. I will obey the law."

In September of this year—November the 14th or whatever day it was—what did he do? He used cocaine. But yet, the government wants you to believe. But, you don't have to believe anybody. It's your choice. You're the judge. You're sitting up there. You're the judge. You can choose who to believe, and who not to believe. Would you trust your house to Frank Freeman?

I told you they would have thieves. What did Frank Freeman tell you he did? He plead guilty. He plead guilty to stealing ten thousand dollars of government money. He plead guilty to it. He stole ten thousand dollars! In his plea agreement, he offered to take a lie detector test. That's what it said in the plea agreement. Has he? No. The government says, "Hey, look, that's okay—you lied to us before. You told us you weren't going to deal drugs anymore. You lied about the money—you lied about all of these things. That's okay. We're not going to give you a polygraph to make sure you're not lying now—but, if you'll tell that story from the witness stand, we'll keep you free."

Did you hear he said he went out to Texas the last time? Where did he say he got the marijuana? He got it from T— he knew T. He'd been to T's house before. Do you recall his saying that? The last trip he went to T's house?

What did Demetric Beans say? "No, they came to my house." Now, we have a liar contest. One of them is telling the truth, and one of them is lying. Maybe both of them are lying, I don't know. Do you know? Can you say beyond a reasonable doubt which one of them is lying? Can you?

You have the information about where Sherman bought that Marquis—he bought it in November of 1998. Check your notes when you go in the back to see when Freeman said he first drove it. He actually drove that car before Sherman bought it, according to his testimony. There are certain things we know because we have documentation of it—and, it's not something constructed for this trial. It's not word of mouth . . . "Well, I didn't mean that, I meant this . . ." We have certain documents.

I ask you to look at when that Marquis was bought. Frank Freeman claimed he was driving it around before Sherman ever bought it. Is that proof beyond a reasonable doubt? Is it? I submit to you it's not. But yet, Ladies and Gentlemen, he's walking around today in our free society after all the drugs he's been involved in with the government letting him. He enjoys the same freedom today that y'all do, that I do—that everybody does.

Is that fair? Is it? Is it fair to put somebody like that on the stand to say, "Believe me!" You know, the only thing that separates us from tyranny is juries—twelve people from the community who are brought into a room like this and says, "No, Government—I don't care! You're not going to run that one by me. I'm not going to believe it. I don't think y'all do, but I'm certainly not going to believe it." That's your job—to separate what's true from what's not true.

In the opening statement, a lot of you are familiar—or, may not have heard—I always do the 'see my hand.' Everybody laughs at it. But, I think it exhibits something—I think it says we're all going to jump to conclusions sometimes, but, yes, I can see your hand. Then I turn at round, and I think that makes juries think, "I'm going to wait for the cross-examination . . ."

That brings me to the expert—of all the experts I met in thirty years of practicing law, my favorite expert was Mr. Soltis. I'm sure he's a brilliant scientist, and he really knows his thing—but, as he told you, all you do in fingerprint analysis is look at the fingerprints. I mean, we're not fools! I can look at fingerprints as well as he can. You can look at fingerprints as well as he can. But, he magnified some fingerprints for us. Look at the fingerprints—we ain't fools! They can bring a high-priced expert in here to say anything they want to, but you got to look at him on the stand. You got to see him. And, the judge is going to tell you, "You don't have to believe him—you can believe your own eyes."

Roderick Ward. Now, you heard what Roderick Ward had to say about things. And, you heard him say he went out there in—I think he got out of jail in '98, I believe he said—and, he went out to Dallas and stayed with Sherman sometime in '98. Sometime in '99. You recall his saying he went out there and stayed at Sherman's house. Well, Sherman's rented to a lady from August '98 until February the 28th of 1999. I guess he wants us to believe that—it's what the agent says when he leased the house, as well as what Roderick Ward said.

Roderick Ward—who is a convicted drug dealer, and who got out of prison in 1996—violated his conditions of release, went back to prison, and got out in 1998. What did he tell you from the witness stand? He said he thought he was going to do twenty years or more. Do you recall that? Now, what does he hope to get? Eighteen to twenty-four months. The government gave him about seventeen to eighteen years' worth of freedom. Now, I don't know how much gold it takes to fill this courtroom for them to buy eighteen years of freedom from any member of jury. But, I submit to you, they couldn't stack up enough in here to pay me for eighteen years. I would do exactly what the government asked me to do. That's what he expects to get out of this . . .

Demetrius Thomas. I kept asking him when he went to Texas the first time, and I tried to get him to relate it to his birthday, which, I believe is May 14th. Check your notes on that, but I believe that's right. He went to Texas the first time, again a couple of weeks later, and he went a third time a month or so later—something like that. He was there within a very short period of time around his birthday.

Now, we can tell whether he's telling the truth about taking that Grand Marquis out to Texas by looking at when it was bought. It wasn't bought until November of 1999. How can he possibly be taking it out to Texas before Mr. Williams ever bought it? Is that possible? I don't think that's possible. I don't think he could have done that. So, why is he telling these lies? Why are these people lying?

For freedom.

They're lying for freedom. They got caught, and they're lying for freedom.

Then we get down to Ms. Beans. Ms. Beans, who is the exotic dancer. Do you recall in the opening statement when Ms. Griffin put all of these names up here on the board? And, you recall she just put them on the board recently. Look at all those names—I told you in the opening statement the linchpin of this case is Demetric Beans. She's the lady who had the connections. She's the lady with the connections . . .

How do we know she had the connections? Because on June the 28th of this year, three or four months ago, she testified before a grand jury. I read this to you yesterday—a juror asked her the question, "You didn't know them prior to Sherman Williams's telling you who they were?" Her answer? "I knew him. I'm the one who introduced them to him, so I didn't know them, but he would tell me of these three guys, which one of them to call."

"You knew these people prior to Sherman Williams knowing them, correct?"

Her answer? Yes. She knew them. She's the one with the drugs. She's the one who knew the drug dealers.

You remember what Ms. Griffin asked her after that? She said, "Well, you told the government the names of these people." Do you recall that? That's why I asked you to listen to cross. She said, "Yes, I told the government the names." On recross, what did she say the names were? Ware, LT, and D. Those are real names . . .

These are drug suppliers, Ladies and Gentlemen. These are people who—whatever you believe in the case—these are the people who are supplying the drugs. These are the higher ups. They were interested in the target of the operation. The target of the operation . . .

She said, "Well, all of these people moved. I don't know anything about them." Blah, blah, etcetera. Is that believable? Would you leave your house for four hours, and let her come in with your valuables there? Would you? I submit you wouldn't.

You know another thing Ms. Beans says when she was asked by the jury, or by Ms. Dow? She was asked, "What's the general procedure when marijuana was at your house to be picked up? Explain to the grand jury generally what would happen . . ." Her answer? "What would happen like what?"

"How would it be picked up, Ms. Beans."

"Well, Shack—he came to pick it up. He had the money. He was the one with the money. Shack."

Is that what she told y'all? Did she tell you that? Did she say Shack was the one? She told the grand jury that, so which is it? This lady is expecting probation for saying it was Sherman Williams today, but, before that, she told the grand jury it was Shack.

She talked about a robbery. She talked about—and, she knew these people—Ware, LT, and D. She knew these people. She said she goes to this house, and she takes cash money into the house of the people she knew. She set it up. She goes to the house, cash money, nobody else goes with her. She comes out, she's not beaten, she's not stabbed, nothing happened to her. She comes out and says, "I got robbed."

Now, that's her friend in there. That's the person with whom she had contact. Do you believe she got robbed? Do you? Do you believe that beyond a reasonable doubt?

I submit to you it's not believable.

Another thing, Ladies and Gentlemen—Ms. Griffin got up here and told you it's about Sherman Williams's greed. How did he run out of money if he didn't run out of money? He still has his money, but it's his greed. He did it all. How many people up here testified to you they ever received a dime from Sherman Williams? Let me tell you something— you want to know the real cruncher? Every single one of them said he didn't pay them anything!

Now, do you believe that people do things for free? Do you? Do you think this was a freebie? That everybody said, "Hey, I'll take time off work. I'll go here, I'll go there for free." But, they couldn't get their stories together, so they said, "I never got any money." Ms. Beans—I never got any money. Thomas—I never got any money. Ward—I never got any money. None of them. Nobody ever got any money. Isn't that amazing to you? Is it believable? Is it believable beyond a reasonable doubt? I submit to you this isn't even close enough for government work. It really isn't . . .

The government brought you a case, and I ask you to use your common sense. Use every day, ordinary common sense. Today is Sherman Williams's day in court, and he is proud to have you as his jury. Tomorrow? It could be any of our day in court, and we would want the same consideration. The same burden of proof. The same presumption of innocence. Would we want those if it were our turn at the table? Would we? I submit to you we would.

Over two hundred years ago, our forefathers fought for this country. They fought the Revolutionary War. I ask you if Mr. Madison, Mr. Jefferson, Mr. Monroe, and Mr. Hancock were sitting here today, listening to this bought and paid for testimony, would there be a tear in their eyes? A tear of shame for what this government has done? Would there?

I want you to—when you leave this courtroom—to look Mr. Madison, Mr. Monroe, and Mr. Washington in the eye and say, "I did the right thing. The government didn't prove, by credible evidence, Sherman Williams is guilty . . ."

Thank you, Ladies and Gentlemen.

THE COURT: Alright. Ms. Griffin . . .

MS. GRIFFIN: Ladies and Gentlemen, you can't look at this video and have any doubt about this case.

(Tape played in open court)

MS. GRIFFIN: You didn't hear Mr. Clark tell you it was Sherman Williams carrying this marijuana out of the apartment. You didn't hear it wasn't Sherman Williams counting every bag, and pinching off the top of it. You didn't hear Mr. Clark tell you Sherman Williams—having bought the Jetta—didn't repossess the Jetta, or he didn't toss the Jetta key when he tripped and finally got caught because he was running.

Use your good common sense—Sherman Williams comes in this courtroom clothed with a presumption, but it has been removed by the government's evidence showing beyond a reasonable doubt he is guilty as charged.

Ladies and Gentlemen, if Sherman Williams didn't put this marijuana in that Jetta when he left that apartment, then you have got to believe there is a marijuana fairy that did it. He walked out of there with it! He had the Jetta key! He's at the end of it, he runs with the Jetta key, and the marijuana is in the Jetta!

Mr. Clark talked to you about freedom—do you think for one minute Sherman Williams doesn't want his freedom? The individuals who testified before you are Sherman Williams's friends. They engaged in criminal activity with him. They don't come and knock on the door before they are caught and say, "Let me tell you about Sherman Williams." That's not reality. They get stopped with drugs, and they tell about not only themselves, but about who else is involved with it.

Sherman Williams wants you to believe these people he hired should go to jail for him rather than take the stand and tell what they did for him. You have to ask yourself if you would go to jail for somebody for whom you were running drugs. Somebody who was taking the profit, who was calling the shots, and who was paying for it. Would you go to jail for him or her? Would you tell about them and about your own participation? Of course, you would.

To believe Sherman Williams isn't guilty, you have to believe Frank Freeman, Trooper Baggett, Sergeant Dunklin, Richard Bryars, David Fagan, John Walls, Demetrius Thomas, William Casper, Roderick Ward, Demetric Beans, Rodney Patrick, Dana Ridenour, and Ruth Kroona lied.

You know that isn't so.

Now, they didn't get the drugs from Dee. Do you recall their telling you a man would come to her apartment and bring them drugs? She was dating Sherman Williams. She was sleeping with Sherman Williams. And, she used her apartment for the transactions to occur. Is she culpable? Yes. She plead guilty, and is awaiting sentencing, just as the others have. They told you their part. They told you they're in this together. Ladies and gentlemen, these people walked out here in shackles for a reason—they took an oath to tell the truth. You—not Mr. Clark, not me, not even the court— decide what they told you is true.

Ladies and Gentlemen, Sherman Williams put a bull's eye on himself by his own behavior. Did you see him walk in that house and say, "Frank, what in the world are you doing having marijuana in here? I can't believe you're selling marijuana, Frank." No. He picked it up, he carried it, and he took it with him because it was his.

Ladies and Gentlemen, you know where justice lies in this case, and you know what's true. Evil triumphs when good men and women like yourselves do nothing. You know where justice lies. You know he is guilty as charged.

By your verdict, you will speak.

THE COURT: Alright. Ladies and Gentlemen, we're going to take a break. I'm going to tell everybody in the courtroom to wait just a minute while the jury leaves to go downstairs. And, I will ask you, Ladies and Gentlemen, to go straight into the jury assembly room. I'm going to have court security officers outside the door there taking orders— so you can have them get a Coke or whatever you can get down there, so other people who are here won't be prohibited from also going down there. But, if everyone would just keep their seats and let the jury go for recess, we'll call you back in about fifteen or twenty minutes. Leave your notepad, and don't talk about the case.

(Jury present)

COURT'S ORAL CHARGE TO THE JURY

THE COURT: Alright, Ladies and Gentlemen, as you are taking your seats, what you'll see is a copy of the Court's instructions that I'm required, by law, to read to you. But, I give juries written copies, as I told you at the beginning of the trial, in order for you to follow along, if you wish. You don't have to—you can simply listen.

It will be your duty to decide whether the government has proved beyond a reasonable doubt the specific facts necessary to find the defendant guilty of the crimes charged in the second, superseding indictment. You must make your decision only on the basis of the testimony, and other evidence presented here during the trial. And, you must not be influenced in any way by either sympathy or prejudice for or against the defendant or the government.

The government has the burden of proving the defendant guilty beyond a reasonable doubt and, if it fails to do so, you must find the defendant not guilty. Thus, while the government's burden of proof is a heavy burden, it's not necessary the defendant's guilt be proved beyond all possible doubt. It's only required the government's proof exclude reasonable doubt concerning the defendant's guilt. And, a reasonable doubt is a real doubt based upon reason and common sense after careful and impartial consideration of all the evidence in the case.

So, it's in your hands, Ladies and Gentlemen. That's the best I can tell you—we're optimistic you will do your job in the manner you swore to do your job.

(RECESS)

THE COURT: Alright. Ladies and Gentlemen—we understand the jury has reached a unanimous verdict on all counts. We will now bring the jury back in, and receive the verdict. Madam Forewoman, has the jury reached a verdict?

THE FOREWOMAN: We have, Your Honor.

VERDICT

THE CLERK: We, the jury, find the defendant, Sherman Williams, guilty as charged in Counts One, Two and Four of the second superseding indictment, and not guilty as charged in Count Three of the second superseding indictment.

THE COURT: Mr. Williams, the jury, having found you guilty of Count One of the indictment, Count Two of the indictment, and Count Four of the indictment, this court judges you to be guilty of those counts of the indictment. And, your sentencing in this matter is set for March the 27th at one o'clock P.M. We will now be in informal recess.

THE COURT: Alright. Counsel, I understand as to the Count Eight forfeiture charge, a resolution of this matter has been reached. Would either counsel like to state what that resolution is?

MS. GRIFFIN: Your Honor, as to Count Eight, Section One, that has already been administered and forfeited to the United States. As to substitute assets, Mr. Williams will pay two hundred and thirty-five thousand to the United States of America. As substitute assets, he will sign a consent degree of forfeiture. And, after consul with his attorney, we will make a decision as to which account of his that comes out of.

THE COURT: Now, Mr. Williams, you have heard what the lawyers and the Court have said. Is that your agreement as well?

THE DEFENDANT: Yes, Sir.

THE COURT: Alright. Then this matter is concluded. I will bring the jury back in and discharge them.

(Jury present)

THE COURT: Alright. You may have your seats, Ladies and Gentlemen. The matter is now concluded—you can go home. The court is adjourned, and you can check out with our thanks, once again.

Thank you. Good evening, and court is adjourned.

THOUGHTS

I wasn't found guilty on all counts, which was my initial thought and feeling. One of the reasons I went to trial was to get released, so I could have an opportunity to re-enter the NFL. I knew if I were going to get a lengthy sentence, then I wouldn't have the opportunity to play in the league again. Playing for the Dallas Cowboys until the 1999 season, I missed only one season in 2000—being found not guilty would enable me to re-enter the NFL for the 2001 season.

After I was found guilty, I already knew my minimum sentence would be five years. So, knowing that, I also knew I wouldn't have the opportunity to re-enter the NFL. That realization was a bitter and sad disappointment, and my spirit was dampened.

It turned out I was right about not being guilty on all charges. At least, the verdict corroborated what I already knew to be true—the prosecution over-stepped the line when presenting their case, and the jury didn't buy it.

I accepted God had different plans for my life without hesitation. But, what a moment of sadness—my passion and dream of being an NFL player was no longer an option.

The reality was stark.

I was going to prison.

CATCHING THE CHAIN

W ell, life of a convicted felon was exactly what it's cracked up to be. I'd been in the county jail in Mobile for close to a year, fighting for my freedom, as well as my NFL career, sentenced by a judge who cheered for me when I ran touchdowns for the University of Alabama— the Honorable Charles Butler.

188 months.

It was a good thing the year I already served was credited to my sentence. Being in the Mobile county jail for a year made me feel like I could handle anything, and the area I was in was protective custody (PC). Every now and then, guys would be connected to my cell, and they tried to explain the difference between going to the state penitentiary versus the federal prison system. At that point, being in the county jail for that long, I didn't really care where I went. I just wanted to be free from the Mobile county jail!

I remember having a conversation with an old white guy who had been to the feds, convicted for flying a plane full of drugs. He was in the system a few times, and he was back with a fresh, new case. He always told me about how the food was so good at the feds—the food in the county jail was like death, itself. Where I was housed, there was lockdown for twenty-three hours, and the other hour was outside of my cell, but still inside the building. So, when other guys would tell me about being outside in the feds, it made me eager to leave the county and get onto the federal prison compound. To me, being outside to smell the fresh air would be a blessing!

While in county jail, I went to bible study on a regular basis just to be out of the cell. It was a strange thing—I was looking forward to going to prison, but, somehow, I didn't think things would get worse than they were at the county jail. Honestly? Those once a week bible studies made me more spiritually conscious than I had ever been before. It was weird because I left a good situation to go to jail—but, I felt when I left the county jail, I would be going to a better place.

After being sentenced, there was another three months' wait to catch what we called 'the chain.' When I talk about 'catching the chain,' it's the process the government uses to transfer prisoners from one institution to another. When in the county jail, there were two ways I could leave the facility. The first and best way was ATW—All The Way out! I imagined hearing my name and ATW called at the end of it, also imagining the feeling of joy and relief. Since I was just sentenced, the only way I would leave the county jail was by catching the chain. The chain rolled on certain days of the week, every other week and, if I didn't get the call for the chain at any given time, then I automatically knew I had at least two weeks in the county.

Agony.

I was anticipating catching the chain within six weeks of sentencing—unfortunately, I didn't get my wish. I was there for twelve weeks after sentencing, waiting to catch the chain. Weeks eight and ten were very disappointing, and I would be up late trying to make sure I didn't miss the call. The chain left in the early morning hours, like a sneak attack. When in week ten I didn't get the call, I damned near threw in the towel. Frustration and anxiety set in, so, when week twelve rolled around, I decided to lie down and not even think about it. Low and behold! I heard, "Sherman Williams, PACK UP!"

It was 2:39 in the morning.

By then, I was one year removed from being a professional athlete, a convicted felon waiting to catch the chain. Some nights I would lie on my back in my cell and pray. I asked God, "Why me?" Other nights, I would lie there and cry, trying to make sense of it all. Many times, I reflected on the words I spoke to the court on the day of my sentencing . . .

I would like to say I feel blessed today to have my family here—to have my friends—showing me so much support throughout these troubled times. And, I want to show my sincere gratitude to my mother for standing by me through everything. My father for being here today. My other friends. David Palmer, and my fiancé, Tasma Scott. I am just blessed to be here today, and in front of you to express these feelings.

It's an unfortunate situation for me to be faced with such difficult circumstances. But, I understand, and I use this time to express my sincere remorse for any wrong doing I have done. But, there have been some things that have been said about me that just aren't true. At the same time, I feel like this experience has took my life from one extreme to another. But, I know it's through God's grace, I will be strong. I will make it through. I will come out, and I will be a better person. I want to say thank you, and may God bless America.

Somehow, that became my whole mindset.

At that point, I knew my life would never be the same. Would I take a turn for the better? Or, worse? Being extremely eager to leave, I picked up on my exercise routine—the only thing about that was trying to find something to eat after a workout since the food served in the county jail was awful. So, I would work out only enough to calm down.

I learned how to hand-wash clothes in the sink with state-issued soap and, since I was still local, my visits were allowed. My Uncle James "Red Dog" Williams came by, and gave me some of his prison knowledge. He served so much time, he could be a certified counselor! In fact, he was in and out of prison for over twenty years. His advice was to forget about the outside world. "Don't think about it," he said, "and your time will go by smoothly."

While he was talking, I wondered how in the world I was going to do that? I would be leaving my kids and fiancé, not to mention my Mother, who was still alive at the time. I'm sure he was giving good advice—it just wasn't good for me.

After visits like that, things started to feel real. Sometimes, I felt as if I were in a bad dream. Could I really be going to federal prison? What should I expect? The only experience I had was going to visit different relatives who were in prison. I tried to reflect on those days, imagining being on the inside—weird thoughts of violence and mayhem. The television versions of prison also promoted scare tactics, and I didn't know if that information would be accurate. After all, it was TV.

Being in PC allowed for a lot of one-on-one time with myself, and I thought it would be much easier to transition to federal prison if I were on the outside. Other times, I thought it would be extremely difficult to show up one day to a prison like, "Let me in, please!" Plus, I would lose out on time served—still, to be out spending time with my family would have been worth it.

The county jail had strict and limited visiting rules, plus no contact. That was one of the things I looked forward to at the prison compound—contact visits. While in the Mobile county jail, all visits were behind glass with a telephone for communicating. One possible reason the jail did that was to eavesdrop on conversations to obtain information they could use in court against inmates.

The only visits privileged to privacy were attorney visits. Whenever, my fiancé, Tasma, visited, we would write on note pads and hold the note up to the glass. Once, Tasma came to visit, telling me about my son playing his first baseball game. At that point, all I could do is cry. I cried so hard, I couldn't stop. Then she started crying, so we ended the visit.

With all the restrictions and limitations, I narrowed down my visit list to my mother and Tasma. There were tons of people who wrote letters in an attempt to be added to the visit list, but I declined them. Some were ex-girlfriends, but with Tasma trying to be there for me, I didn't want her to feel insulted. During the time waiting to catch the chain, an entire year passed since I was with Tasma physically—that was one of the toughest things about the whole situation. Don't get me wrong—I love my kids, and I missed my mother dearly, but I needed that woman's touch. Having a more spiritual state of mind made me more aware of my feelings.

Over the course of a year in the metro, I accumulated a stockpile of files, mail, phone numbers, books, bibles, etc. I was told when I catch the chain, all I would be allowed to carry was one sheet of paper with my property listed on it. So, I began to downsize, sending court documents home to my mother's house. I kept up with every person who reached out to me during my incarceration, keeping all contact information. I planned to reach out to everyone to thank them once I made it to the prison yard.

That turned out to be a very wise decision because one of the people in that pile was a very special young lady named Georgiana Threats—now known as Georgiana Williams.

A fifteen-year prison sentence can lead you down a road with a lot of twist and turns. Ups and downs. Highs and lows. For me, the journey to federal prison had just begun. I tried to keep a level head and an open mind, but, I really had no way to prepare for the journey that prison life was about to take me on . . .

PRELUDE

Crimson Cowboy, Volume III will give you a real, up close and personal journey of the trials and triumphs of a former State, National, and Super Bowl champion who fell from grace. A life diminished to prison yard flag football championships, hole time, drug use and prison riots, as well as a true spiritual transformation.

One can only wonder how a life in federal prison can provide peace between the lines . . .

STAY TUNED!

PROFESSIONAL ACKNOWLEDGMENTS

CHRYSALIS PUBLISHING AUTHOR SERVICES

L.A. O'Neil, Editor
chrysalispub@gmail.com
www.chrysalis-pub.com

HIGH MOUNTAIN DESIGN

Wyatt Ilsley, Cover Design
HIGH MOUNTAIN DESIGN
hmdesign89@gmail.com

PHOTOGRAPHY

Dr. Resia Thornton Brooks, Photographer
Providence Photography
resia@providencepics.com

Made in the USA
Columbia, SC
16 August 2019